THE U.S. GOVERNMENT GUIDE TO

SURVIVING TERRORISM

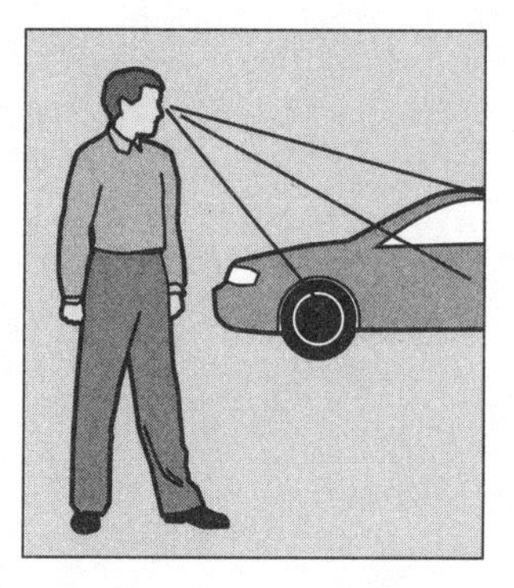

This edition published by Barnes & Noble, Inc.
by arrangement with Quirk Packaging, Inc.
2003 Barnes & Noble
ISBN 0-7607-4891-8

Designed by Niloo Tehranchi and Christine Licata

M 10 9 8 7 6 5 4 3 2 1

THE U.S. GOVERNMENT GUIDE TO
SURVIVING TERRORISM

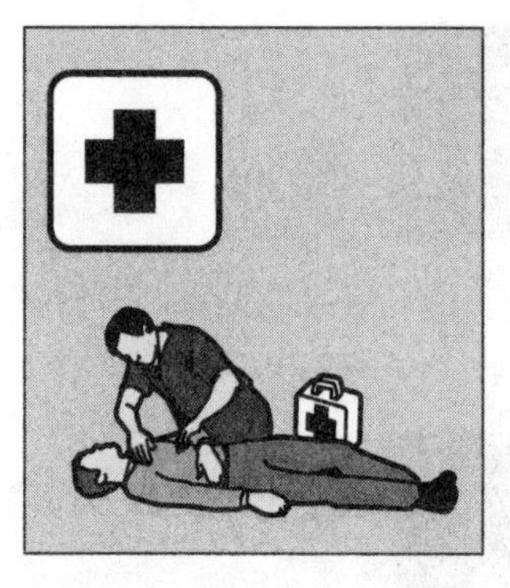

Introduction by H. Keith Melton
Centre for Counterterrorism Studies

CONTENTS

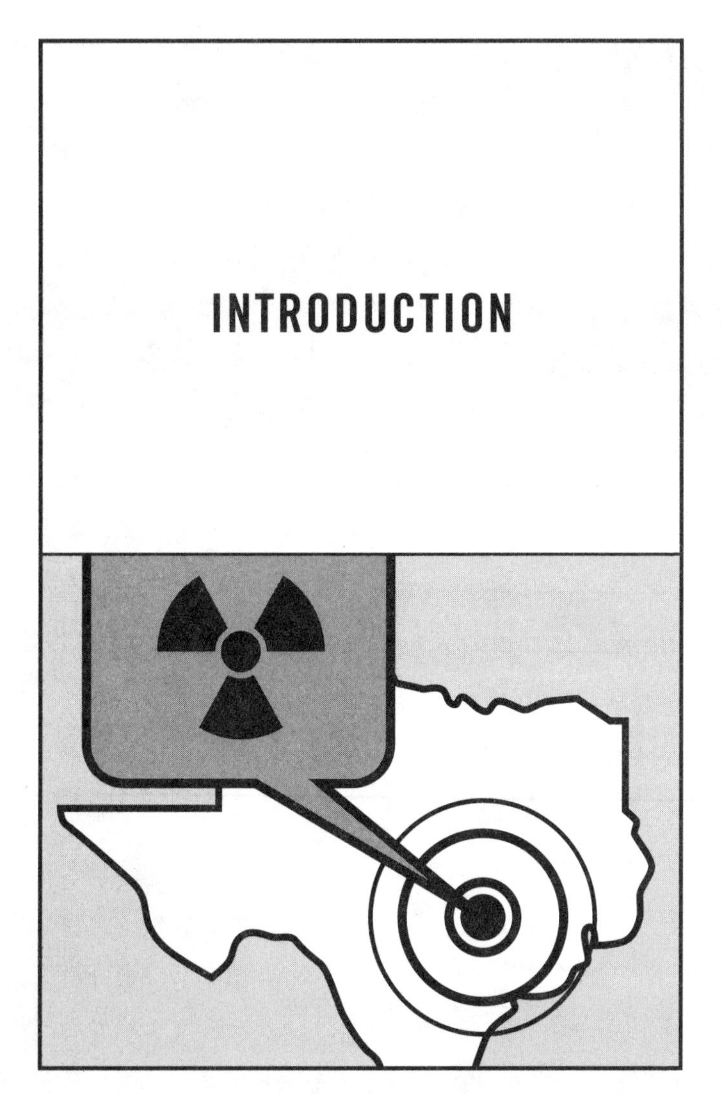
INTRODUCTION

Though we live in dangerous times, there hasn't been a period in the last few hundred years when our world was ever truly peaceful. Even in the best, or most peaceful, of times there have always been "hot spots" of revolution, civil wars, ethnic rivalries, and religious extremism. It was hoped, perhaps naively, that the end of the Cold War would usher in an era of peace, prosperity and global harmony. Unfortunately, the regional conflicts that grew out of the collapse of the Soviet Union and the subsequent rise of radical Islamic fundamentalism have instead created a world that may be even more dangerous!

In 1998 former Director of Central Intelligence James Woolsey summarized the instability of the post-Cold War era as follows:

> It is as if we were struggling with a large dragon for forty-five years, killed it, and then found ourselves in a jungle full of poisonous snakes—and the snakes are much harder to keep track of than the dragon ever was.

Gone is the familiar and predictable world that we had become accustomed to in which the two superpowers, or "dragons", orchestrated, managed, and often were able to contain the various conflicts that threatened to boil over around the globe. With the other "dragon" slain, we are now confronting the many "poisonous snakes" that inhabit an increasing number of regional hot spots. Director Woolsey was correct to point out that, in comparison, it was in many ways easier "to keep track of the dragon."

No longer can the intelligence and security services of the United States and her allies limit their predictions and potential courses of action to events that are "likely" to happen, but rather must now address the infinitely more difficult question of what might happen, and there are myriad possiblities. To understand the nature of impending threats confronting the United States, we must, insofar as possible, adopt the bizarre mentality of a follower of Osama Bin Laden, or North Korea's Kim Jong Il, and ask, Is there an act of terror that a fanatic would not commit? Unfortunately, the answer is an emphatic "*no!*" Radical, violent religious fundamentalists and rogue nations don't understand restraint; the scope of their attacks is limited only by the availability of the weapons at hand. If weapons of mass destruction aren't available, they'll reach for the next most powerful weapon and willingly sacrifice their lives to cause the greatest possible devastation.

Terrorists typically utilize a technique known as "asymmetrical warfare" wherein a numerically smaller and weaker group of attackers adopt those weapons and tactics that offer them the best advantage against the larger and stronger opponent. In the case of the attacks that occurred on September 11, 2001, the terrorists utilized box-cutters to gain control of fully laden jet liners; then they used the airplanes as weapons to be crashed into their targets. The audacity and scale of these attacks found the United States unprepared; our external defenses were still configured to fight a conventional war against an opponent of known size on a comprehensible battlefield. Conversely, our internal defenses, weakened by years of inadequate funding, were shown to be inadequate. In addition, our porous borders had allowed the terrorists behind these attacks to enter and roam the country freely.

The goals of terrorists are the same everywhere and have changed very little in hundreds of years: Kill one person, wound several, and frighten thousands. As a result, the greatest and most far reaching damage from a terrorist attack usually comes *after* the incident, in the form of public panic.

Today's terrifying reality is that because of the collapse of the Soviet Union, and the financial support of terrorist sympathizers, the materials for weapons of mass destruction (nuclear, biological, or chemical) may soon, if not already, be in the hands of terrorists. The use of any of these weapons in a future terrorist attack would likely result in global chaos.

Despite all this bad news, are there precautions that the average American citizen can take to survive a terrorist attack? Yes, of course, and the precautions begin with each of us raising and maintaining a state of alertness. Unfortunately though, alertness alone is inadequate. You can be alert, but to what? Unless you know and understand the types of threats you might face, you can be alert, and still be unprepared. The key, then, is to combine alertness with knowledge.

The United States government has written detailed training manuals for members of the military and intelligence services on surviving terrorist attacks. We've searched out the very best of these publications and combined them to provide you with a single guidebook on how to survive.

In Chapter 1 you can review the overall pattern of global terrorism and in Chapter 2 you can begin to identify the types of attacks that are most likely to threaten you and your family. Recognizing the variables about where you live, work, and travel will help you better understand and prioritize the threats you might encounter. For example, if you never travel abroad, the likelihood of being kidnapped and taken hostage is probably remote. Conversely, your vulnerability to a "dirty bomb" attack increases if you live within, or frequently travel to, a major city such as Washington, DC or New York. Understanding your exposure to different types of threats will help you determine your own "threat profile". Once you understand what types of threats you are likeliest to face, you will be ready to learn how to respond and survive each type of attack.

Chapter 3 focuses on preventing and preparing for attacks, beginning with an important overview of home security. You'll learn the steps necessary to create a safe room at home and how to make a family plan that is personalized for you and your lifestyle. Would you have detected the infamous "anthrax letters" in 2001 if you found them inside your mailbox? In this chapter you'll learn the telltale characteristics that will enable you to spot suspicious letters and parcels *before you open them.*

Do you travel abroad? If so, Chapter 3 also provides a wealth of important information for travelers, including tips on preparations and plans for safe travel that should be undertaken *before* you leave home! Understanding your vulnerabilities while in the air, arriving at a foreign airport, getting to the hotel, and using public transportation, as well as being identified as an American and targeted because of your wealth or perceived importance, is crucial to your safe return.

Chapter 3 also warns you that if you live abroad, automobiles parked on a public street make inviting targets for concealed explosive devices. Would you be able to tell if your automobile had been tampered with while parked? Could there be a bomb planted beneath the driver's seat just waiting for you to climb in and sit down? You'll learn the reasons to avoid parking your automobile in vulnerable locations and the proper procedures to conduct a through search of your vehicle before opening the door.

Each type of terrorist attack has a unique "signature" and requires a different response. The steps you'll take to survive a biological attack in a major urban area are very different from those you'll need to follow to protect against a radioactive attack or the fallout following an attack on a nearby nuclear power plant. In Chapter 4, you'll learn how to recognize the different types of terrorist attacks and to answer the most pressing questions that follow: Do I stay where I am or leave? Which is safer? Where do I go? What if my family is separated at the time of the attack? How do we gather? Reacting to a terrorist attack quickly and correctly can save the lives of you and your loved ones.

Of the ten most dangerous countries in the world for kidnappings, seven are in the Americas and are located south of the United States. If you are surprised that you haven't read about these alarming statistics, there is a logical explanation: It's bad for tourism, and often the countries involved cover up the occurrences of kidnappings and crimes against travelers as a matter of national survival. If you travel south of the United States, the tips in Chapter 5 are necessary for you and your family to minimize the risks of being taken hostage. And should you become a hostage, you'll learn the strategies necessary to survive.

In the Appendices, you will find sources of further information, as well as several handy checklists to aid you in assembling your own information. Also useful are templates for wallet cards that you and your family members can carry at all times—these cards will contain necessary information on your family plan.

Is the terrorist threat "real enough" that extraordinary measures for survival may be necessary? The answer is an unqualified "*yes!*" Communication intercepts about impending terrorist attacks against the United States and her allies are received daily. The question is not *if* future attacks will occur, but rather *when* and *where* the next attack will happen. If you don't take precautions, you may become a victim! You've been wise enough to purchase this manual. Now, use it thoughtfully and deliberately to prepare each member of your family with the information they will need to survive.

H. Keith Melton
The Centre for Counterterrorism Studies

PART ONE

WHAT IS TERRORISM?

CHAPTER 1

TERRORISM DEFINED

The United States Department of Defense defines terrorism as "the calculated use of unlawful violence or threat of unlawful violence to inculcate fear; intended to coerce or to intimidate governments or societies in the pursuit of goals that are generally political, religious, or ideological." Within this definition are three key elements: violence, fear, and intimidation. Each element produces terror in its victims.

Objectives of Terrorism

Terrorism is a criminal act that influences an audience beyond the immediate victim. The strategy of terrorists is to commit acts of violence that draw the attention of the local populace, the government (sometimes more than one government), and the world to their cause. Terrorists plan attacks to obtain the greatest publicity, choosing targets that symbolize what they oppose. The effectiveness of the terrorist act lies not in the act itself, but in the public's or the government's reaction to the act.

For example, at the 1972 Munich Olympics, the Black September Organization killed 11 Israelis. The murdered Israelis were the immediate victims, but the true target was the estimated 1 billion people watching the televised event.

The Black September Organization used the high visibility of the Olympics to publicize its views on the plight of Palestinian refugees.

Similarly, in October 1983, Middle Eastern terrorists bombed the Marine Battalion Landing Team Headquarters at Beirut International Airport. Their immediate victims were the 241 U.S. military personnel who were killed and more than 100 others who were wounded. The true targets were the American people and the U.S. Congress. This one act of violence led to the U.S. decision that withdrawl of the Marines from Beirut was for the best, and was therefore considered a terrorist success.

On September 11, 2001, terrorists skyjacked four U.S. commercial planes. They crashed two planes into the World Trade Center in New York City and one into the Pentagon in Washington, D.C. The fourth plane crashed in a field in western Pennsylvania; its target remains unknown. These terrorist attacks inflicted serious loss of life—more than 3,000 people were killed—by destroying the World Trade Center towers and part of the Pentagon building. They were designed to strike a blow at the American willand its economic and military structure. Although the attacks succeeded in hitting their targets, they also galvanized the will of the American public to take political, financial, and military actions to combat terrorism.

There are three perspectives of terrorism: the terrorist's, the victim's, and the general public's. Many terrorists would like to see widespread acceptance of the view indicated by the phrase "one man's terrorist is another man's freedom fighter." Terrorists do not see themselves as evil. They believe they are legitimate combatants, fighting for what they believe in, by whatever means possible. A victim of a terrorist act sees the terrorist as a criminal with no regard for human life. The general public's view is the most unstable. Terrorists take great pains to foster a Robin Hood image in hopes of swaying public opinion to their cause.

Today's Threat—Types of Terrorists

Many areas of the world are currently experiencing great political, economic, and social unrest. The reasons for this unrest can be seen in conflicts with neighboring states, internal strife, dissatisfaction with governments in power, unconstrained population growth, declining resources, culture clashes, and ethnic and religious hatreds. This unrest has spawned numerous groups that lack the means to have their grievances solved by their own governments, through the normal political processes. Sometimes, these groups resort to terrorism to achieve their aims. Generally, these aims stem from political ideology, nationalism, religion, or special interests. Over the past twenty years, terrorists have claimed political or religious reasons for their extremely violent acts.

Political ideology ranges from the far left to the far right. For example, the far left can consist of groups such as Marxists and Leninists who propose a revolution of workers led by a revolutionary elite. On the far right there may be dictatorships that believe in a merging of state and business or religious leadership.

Nationalism is the devotion to the interests or culture of a group of people or a nation. Typically, nationalists share a common ethnic background and wish to establish or regain a homeland.

Religious extremists often reject the authority of secular governments and view legal systems that are not based on their religious beliefs as illegitimate. They often view modernization efforts as corrupting influences on traditional culture.

Special interest groups include people on the radical fringe of many legitimate causes such as the "right-to-life" movement, or the animal rights movement. Many members of these movements believe that violence is morally justifiable to achieve their goals.

INTENTIONS OF TERRORIST GROUPS

While their overall goal might be to effect large-scale political or ideological change, terrorists usually have numerous short-term goals attached to each of their actions. These may include the following:

- To produce widespread fear.
- To obtain worldwide, national, or local recognition for their cause by attracting the attention of the media.
- To harass, weaken, or embarrass government security forces so that the government overreacts and appears repressive.
- To steal or extort money and equipment, especially weapons and ammunition.
- To destroy facilities or disrupt lines of communication in order to create doubt that the government can provide for and protect its citizens.
- To discourage foreign investments, tourism, or assistance programs that can affect the target country's economy and support of the government in power.

- To influence government decisions, legislation, or other critical decisions.
- To free prisoners.
- To satisfy vengeance.
- To turn the tide in a guerrilla war by forcing government security forces to concentrate their efforts in urban areas. This allows the terrorist groups to establish themselves among the local populace in rural areas.

GENERAL CHARACTERISTICS OF TERRORIST GROUPS

Most terrorist groups share certain characteristics:

- They seek to intimidate by promoting fear.
- Generally, they are militarily weaker than the governments they fight (though some groups have been able to obtain advanced weaponry, e.g., tanks, in limited quantities).
- They employ unconventional warfare tactics; terrorists may be trained in physical and mental preparation, weapons and explosives, political and religious indoctrination, combat tactics, intelligence gathering, psychological warfare, survival, and communications.

- They do not equate tactical success with mission success. A specific terrorist act may not achieve its desired results, but a terrorist may still view the act as successful if it publicizes the cause.
- They are usually urban-based and highly mobile. If urban-based, terrorists have access to mass transportation (e.g., airplanes, ships, railroads, and subways). Terrorist groups with international contacts may also have access to forged passports and safe havens in countries other than their home base.
- Generally, they organize and operate clandestinely in cells of three to five members. A cell may have contact only with another cell or only with the next step up in the command hierarchy. Therefore, the capture of one or more terrorists rarely compromises the identity or plans of the entire organization.

CHAPTER 2

TYPES OF TERRORIST ATTACKS

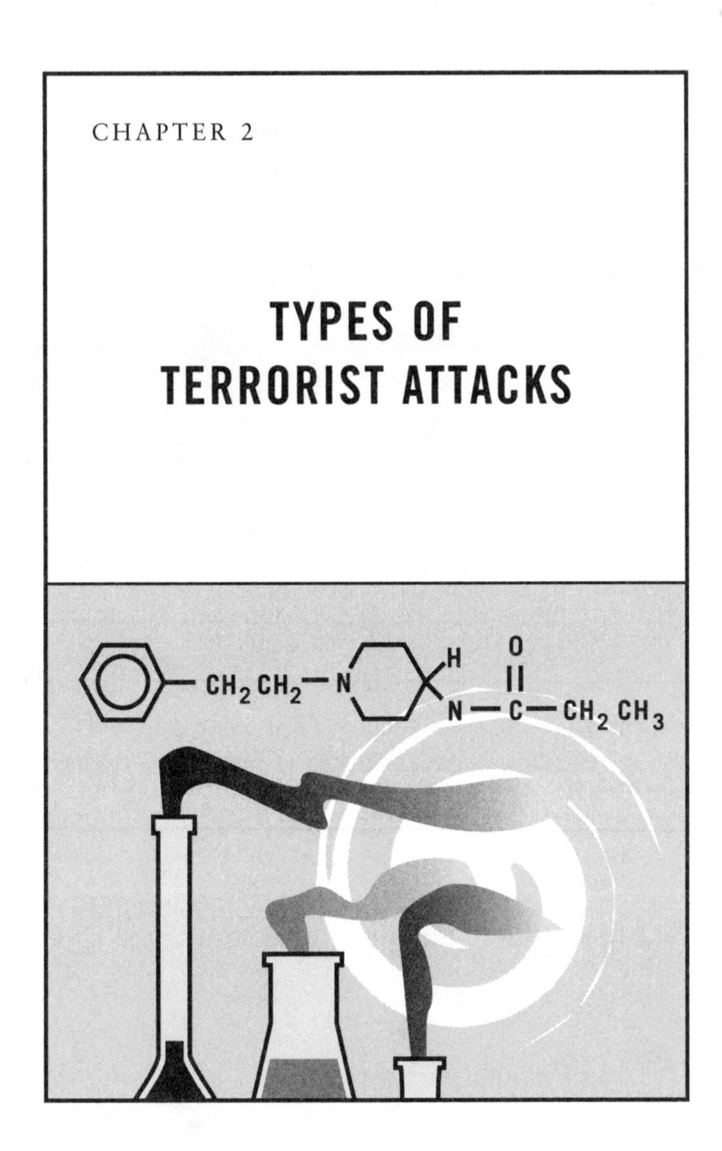

Terrorist threats come in many forms, each featuring different effects and requiring different responses. It is important to be able to recognize and plan for each type of threat, so that you can best prepare for all contingencies. This chapter features descriptions of the various kinds of terrorist actions. For the best ways to prepare for and respond to these attacks, see *Part Two: How Can I Protect Myself and My Family?*

Recently, there has been much talk, and even military action, about so-called weapons of mass destruction (WMD), devices that use nuclear, biological, and chemical (NBC) agents. Traditionally, NBC attacks have been rare. Today, however, a number of nations are involved in arms races with neighboring countries because they view the development of WMD as a key deterrent of attack by hostile neighbors. The increased development of WMD also increases the potential for terrorist groups to gain access to these weapons. Many people believe that if this trend continues, terrorists' access to WMD will grow because unstable nations or states may fail to safeguard their stockpiles from accidental losses, illicit sales, or outright theft or seizure.

Determined and well-funded terrorist groups can also gain access to WMD through covert independent research efforts or by hiring skilled professionals to construct them.

Although an explosive nuclear device is believed to be beyond the scope of most terrorist groups, biological, chemical, or radiological dispersion weapons (which use nuclear contaminants) are not. In addition, terrorists' dependence on tried-and-true tactics—bombings, hijackings, armed attacks, and kidnappings—has not waned.

Biological Threat

A biological attack is the deliberate release of germs or other biological substances that make people sick. Such substances can gain access to the body by being inhaled, through a cut in the skin, or by being eaten. Some biological agents, such as anthrax, do not cause contagious diseases. Others, like the smallpox virus, can result in diseases that spread from person to person.

Unlike an explosion, a biological attack may or may not be immediately obvious. In October 2001, several letters were mailed to selected members of the U.S. government and media personalities. Those letters contained the biological agent anthrax. In large amounts or even small amounts widely distributed, such biological agents can be a weapon of mass destruction. Fear of these biological agents can create as much terrorist value as their actual deployment.

While it is possible that you will see signs of a biological attack, as was sometimes the case with the anthrax mailings, it is perhaps more likely that local health care workers will report a pattern of unusual illness or there will be a wave of sick people seeking emergency medical attention. You will probably learn of the danger through an emergency radio or television broadcast or some other signal used in your community. Perhaps you will get a phone call, or emergency response workers will go door-to-door informing people and investigating the effect on public health.

Chemical Threat

A chemical attack is the deliberate release of a toxic gas, liquid, or solid that can poison people and the environment. Chemical attacks are less obvious than bombs or arson, as they don't usually cause intense damage to property, but they are more readily apparent than biological attacks. One tragic example of the use of chemical agents for a terrorist act occurred on March 20, 1995, when operatives of the Japanese religious cult Aum Shinrikyo, or Supreme Truth, released the nerve agent sarin in the Tokyo subway system, resulting in 12 deaths and thousands of injuries.

Chemical agents are generally liquids, often aerosolized

(stored under pressure as a fine mist) for easier distribution among a populace. Although some chemical effects are delayed, most induce an immediate response. There are many different chemical agents that provide weapon potential for terrorists, and each has its own specific effects. Nonetheless, the following broad generalizations can be made:

- Inhalation is the most likely method of delivery, though food or water contamination is possible.
- Many likely agents are heavier than air and will tend to stay close to the ground. Chemical agents tend to present an immediate noticeable effect.
- Most chemical agents that present an inhalation hazard will break down fairly rapidly when exposed to sun, diluted with water, or dissipated in high winds.
- No matter what agent has been used or what the particular concentration is, evacuation is always advisable unless you are properly equipped with an appropriate breathing device and protective clothing.

Nuclear Blast

A nuclear blast is an explosion featuring intense light and heat, a damaging pressure wave, and the spreading of radioactive material, which can contaminate the air, water, and ground for miles around. While experts may predict that a nuclear attack is currently less likely than other kinds of terrorist assaults, terrorism is, by its nature, unpredictable.

A nuclear explosion has both immediate and long-term effects: The blast can cause incredible damage to property, land, and people, and the resulting radiation can make people sick and contaminate food and arable land, as well as the air and physical materials.

Radiation Threat ("Dirty Bomb")

A radiation threat, often called a "dirty bomb," is the use of common explosives to spread radioactive materials over a targeted area. It is not a nuclear blast. The force of the explosion and radioactive contamination will be more localized. While the blast will be immediately obvious, the presence of radiation may not be clearly defined until trained personnel with specialized equipment are on the scene.

Bombings

Bombings are the most common type of terrorist act. Typically, improvised explosive devices are inexpensive and easy to make. Today's devices are smaller and harder to detect than ever, and they can be extremely destructive. On August 7, 1998, for example, two American embassies in Africa were bombed. More than 200 people were killed, including twelve American citizens, and over 5,000 civilians were injured.

Terrorists can also use materials readily available to the average consumer to construct a bomb. On April 19, 1995, for example, 168 people were killed when an improvised explosive device was set off at the Murrah Federal Building in Oklahoma City, Oklahoma.

In the case of the attacks in the United States on September 11, 2001, terrorists skyjacked commercial planes, laden with full fuel tanks, to fly them into buildings as guided missiles or massive flying bombs. This awakened the world to a new level of terrorist bombing potentiall.

Vehicles packed with explosives have a long history among terrorists. They were used to kill scores of U.S. Marines in Lebanon in 1983 and are a common weapon in the Middle East today.

However, bombings don't have to cause large-scale damage or great numbers of deaths to be effective terror weapons. Letter bombs are often used to kill individuals or to destroy small buildings or parts of buildings.

Hijackings and Skyjackings

Hijacking is the seizure by force of a surface vehicle, its passengers, and/or its cargo. Skyjacking is the taking of an aircraft, this creates a mobile hostage situation, providing terrorists with captives from many nations and drawing heavy media attention. Skyjacking also provides mobility; with an aircraft filled with hostages, terrorists have both transport to a country that supports their cause and a human shield to protect them on their trip. This makes retaliation very difficult.

The attacks on and taking of the commercial airplanes in the United States that occured on September 11, 2001, were not, strictly speaking, skyjackings. The terrorists' intent was not to create a hostage situation, but to turn the aircraft into flying bombs.

Arson and Firebombs

Incendiary devices are cheap to make and easy to hide. Arson and firebombings are easily conducted by terrorist groups or individuals who are not very well-organized, well-equipped, or well-trained. Arson and firebombings against utilities, hotels, government buildings, or industrial centers are commonly conducted by terrorists to show that the ruling government is incapable of maintaining order.

Armed Attacks and Assassinations

Armed attacks include raids and ambushes. An assassination is the killing of a selected victim, usually using a bomb or small arms. Drive-by shootings are a common technique employed by loosely organized terrorist groups. Historically, terrorists have assassinated specific individuals for psychological effect or to undermine the workings of a government.

Kidnappings and Hostage-Takings

Terrorists use kidnappings and hostage-takings to establish bargaining positions and to elicit publicity. Although kidnapping is one of the most difficult acts for a terrorist group to accomplish, if it is successful, it can gain terrorists money, release of jailed comrades, and publicity for an extended period of time.

Hostage-taking involves the seizure of a facility or location and the capture of usually innocent people. Unlike a kidnapping, a hostage-taking provokes a confrontation. It forces authorities either to make dramatic decisions or to comply with the terrorists' demands. Hostage-taking is overt and designed to attract and hold media attention. The terrorists' intended target is the audience affected by the hostage's confinement, not the hostage himself. (For a detailed discussion of hostage-takings, see *Chapter 5*.)

Other Types of Attacks

In addition to the acts above, numerous other types of violence exist under the framework of terrorism. Terrorist groups conduct maimings against their own people as a form of punishment for security violations, defections, or informing. Terrorist organizations also conduct robberies and extortion when they need to finance their acts and are without sponsorship from sympathetic nations.

The newest type of attack maybe cyberterrorism, which targets computer networks. Cyberterrorism allows terrorists to conduct their operations with little or no risk to themselves. It also provides an opportunity to disrupt or destroy networks and computers, interrupting key government or business-related activities. Although this type of terrorism lacks a high profile compared to other types of attacks, its impact can be just as destructive, sometimes more so.

PART TWO

HOW CAN I PROTECT MYSELF AND MY FAMILY?

CHAPTER 3

PREPARATION: BEFORE THE ATTACK

Now that you know how to distinguish the various types of attacks that may occur, you can consider how best to plan for their eventuality. The threats and their likelihood are different when you are at home and when you are traveling—if a terrorist incident occurs domestically, it will most likely be a WMD attack or a bombing of some kind—but the policy of prevention and response is the same no matter where you are: Be informed, be alert, and be ready.

Types of Targets

Terrorists prefer a target that involves little risk and a high probability of success. Terrorists evaluate a target's security profile, predictability, and value. The target's value is determined by its importance and possible benefits gained from an attack. Once a target has been evaluated by terrorists, it is labeled in the terrorist's mind as either a soft or a hard target. The target issue is a much greater concern for the average citizen when you are abroad than when you are home. It should be your goal to put yourself firmly in the latter category.

SOFT TARGETS

Soft targets are accessible, predictable, and unaware. They make it easy for strangers to access their private information (e.g., phone numbers, addresses, and schedules). Soft targets follow consistent routines at home and at work, allowing terrorists to predict movements in advance. Soft targets are unaware of their surroundings and do not employ individual protective measures.

HARD TARGETS

Hard targets are inaccessible, unpredictable, and aware. They make it difficult for terrorists to gain access to themselves or their families. Hard targets consciously vary their routines and avoid setting patterns in their daily lives. They are security-conscious and aware of their surroundings, and they proactively adhere to individual protective measures. Hard targets do not

- Put their names on mailboxes or exterior walls of their homes.
- Run or walk daily at the same time of day or to the same place.
- Wash cars, mow lawns, or have family cookouts the

same day every week.

- Shop the same day of each week at the same store.
- Travel to and from home on the same route and at the same time every day.
- Attend church services at the same time of day and place each week.
- Sit in the same seat in a vehicle, at a restaurant, at church, or in other public settings.
- Arrive at work, go to lunch, or depart work at the same time every day.
- Pick up the newspaper or mail at the same time every day.
- Walk or feed the dog along the same route or at the same time every day.
- Patronize the same restaurants or bars or, when abroad, patronize only American restaurants or bars.
- Park vehicles in the same area at church, social events, and various other public gatherings.
- Earn the reputation of always lending a helping hand, e.g., aiding victims at roadside accidents.

At Home

When you are home in the United States, it is unlikely, in our current situation, that you will face any sort of home invasion or vehicular attack by foreign terrorists. However, the situation is rapidly changing, and domestic terrorism has grown in the last several years—from the activities of the Unabomber between 1978 and 1993 to the bombing of the Murrah Federal Building in Oklahoma City in 1995—so it is best to know how to prevent these sorts of situations and how to protect yourself should they occur. Furthermore, the following is also good advice for keeping more common criminals at bay.

HOME SECURITY

The following section provides some basic information on how to make your home a hard target. Develop a security plan that includes the following:

Operations Security. Don't provide information to potential terrorists or criminals via the mail, phone, computer or trashcan. Shred documents before placing them in the garbage, or burn them if you have the ability. Take precautions to ensure that your computer and phone are secure; consult a technology expert.

Outer Security. Use available assets (local shop owners, neighbors, domestic employees, guards, family, etc.)

to detect potential surveillance.

Inner Security. Establish a warning system with pets, alarms, and motion sensors.

Barriers. Consider putting up fences and walls; always lock doors and windows; create secure rooms that you can go to in an emergency.

Deterrent/Response Systems. Consider guards, perhaps in the form of pets, and weapons (but make sure you are properly licensed). Be sure also to have fire extinguishers, and get them checked regularly by your local fire department.

Communications. Make sure your communications systems are secure. Set up intercoms and have radios on hand for internal use. Install audible alarms and security systems linked to your local law enforcement or a private security force.

- Don't place your name in a public phone directory.
- If you receive obscene, threatening or annoying phone calls or an unusual number of wrong or silent callers, report this to the police. Use caller ID or call blocking, if available.
- Answer the phone without providing any personal information. Be especially cautious when sending personal information over the Internet.

- Report any interruption or unusual interference with phone, electrical, or computer service. This could be the first indication of your phone line being "bugged."
- Memorize emergency telephone numbers—police, fire department, hospital, and ambulance—and also place them on the telephone. If possible, program the numbers into your phone.
- Keep a cellular phone charged and available, particularly at night.

GENERAL

- Instruct your family and associates not to provide strangers with information about you or your family.
- Avoid giving unnecessary personal details to anyone.
- Be alert to strangers who have no business being near your property. Report all suspicious persons to local law enforcement; attempt to provide a complete description. If there is a suspicious vehicle involved, take the license number and report that as well.
- Vary daily routines, such as departure times and routes to and from work, to avoid habitual patterns.
- Refuse to meet with strangers outside your workplace.
- Always advise associates or family members of your

destination and the anticipated time of arrival when leaving the office or home.

- Don't open doors to strangers.
- Be cautious about giving out information regarding family travel plans or security measures and procedures.
- Restrict the possession of house keys. Change or re-key locks as well as the security code in the garage door opener when you move in or when a key is lost or stolen. Never leave a house or trunk key with your ignition key while your car is being serviced or parked by an attendant.
- Lock all entrances at night, including the garage. Keep the house locked, even if you are at home. Keep all window curtains and blinds tightly closed after sundown.
- Be cautious about peddlers and strangers.
- Don't open doors to strangers. Observe them through a peephole. Establish procedures for accepting deliveries: verify identities of delivery people, check the identity of the deliverer with the appropriate dispatcher, refuse all unexpected packages.
- Allow maintenance work only on a scheduled basis, unless a clear emergency exists. Be alert to people disguised as public utility crews, road workers, vendors etc., who might station themselves near the house to observe activities and gather information.

- Install lighting all around the house and yard; link to timers and sensors.
- Ensure that door frames, doors, locks, and bolts are of solid construction. Ensure that door hinges exposed to outside of house are pinned or spot-welded to prevent removal of the hinge bolt.
- Ensure that fuse boxes are secure from tampering.
- Remove all trees, poles, ladders, etc., that might help an intruder scale fences, or walls or gain access to second-floor windows. Remove dense foliage or shrubbery near gates, garages, windows, or doors that might conceal an intruder.
- Install intrusion detection, smoke, and fire alarms. Ensure that intrusion detection alarms cover both the perimeter (doors and windows) and interior (motion and/or glass break sensors). Have the alarms monitored through a reputable security service or ur local police department. Train family members to use and to test the alarms regularly.
- If possible, select and prepare an interior safe room for use in case of emergencies. The safe room should have a sturdy door with a lock and an emergency exit, if possible. Bathrooms on upper floors are generally good safe rooms.
- Store emergency and first aid supplies in the safe

room. Bars or grillwork on safe room windows should be locked from the inside to expedite escape.

- Keep keys to locks and a rope or chain ladder to ease escape.

SECURITY PRECAUTIONS WHEN YOU'RE AWAY

- Leave the house with a lived-in look: Use a timer to turn lights on and off at varying times and locations. Ask neighbors to adjust blinds and draperies and to pick up newspapers and mail. Schedule regular lawn work.
- Stop deliveries of mail, or have it forwarded to a neighbor's home.
- Don't leave notes on doors.
- Don't hide keys outside house.
- Leave radio on.
- Hide valuables.
- Notify the police or a trusted neighbor of your absence.
- Ask a trusted friend or neighbor to periodically check your residence.

LETTER BOMBS AND BIOLOGICAL MAILINGS

Heightened personal security involves treating any suspicious-looking mail (letter or package) as a bomb or a potential biological threat. If you think any mail is suspicious, contact the police or appropriate security officials and let them investigate. Do not attempt to handle the mail yourself. You should examine your mail for the following suspicious features:

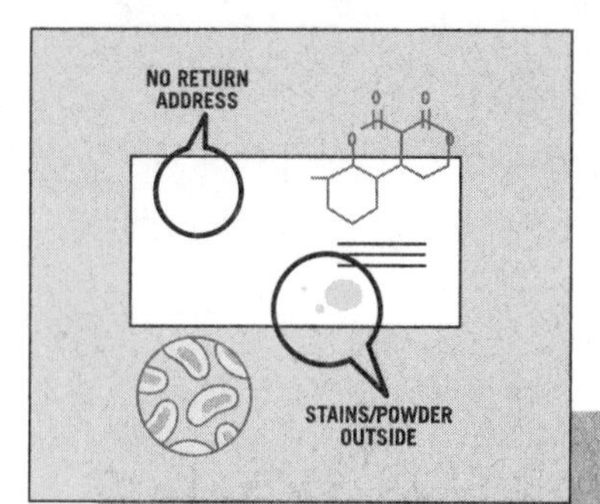

- It is from a stranger or an unknown place?
- Is the return address missing?
- Is there an excessive amount of postage?
- Is the size excessive or unusual?
- Does it have external wires or strings that protrude?
- Is the spelling correct?
- Does the return address match the place of postmark?
- Does it smell peculiar?
- Is it unusually heavy or light?

- Is it unbalanced (lopsided)?
- Are there any oily, sticky, or powdery substances on the outside of the letter or package?
- Does it have springiness on the top, bottom or sides?

You should use the following guidelines if you suspect that a piece of mail contains a bomb or biological agent:

- Don't panic.
- Do not shake the empty contents of any suspicious envelope or package. If any powder or substance leaks out, do not attempt to clean it up.
- Never cut tape, strings, or other wrappings on a suspect package or immerse a suspected letter or package in water. Either action could cause an enclosed explosive device to detonate.
- Place the envelope or package in a plastic bag or some other type of container to prevent leakage of the contents. (If you do not have a container, cover the mail and do not remove the cover. If powder or any other substance has already leaked out, cover that also. You can cover the mail with clothing, paper, trash cans, etc.)
- Leave the room and close the door. Secure the area to prevent others from entering.
- Wash your hands with soap and water to prevent the spread

of any biological agent to your skin or respiratory system.

- Report the incident to authorities. If at home, dial 911 and inform your local law enforcement agency. If at work, report the occurence to the local law enforcement agency and notify your building security official or an available supervisor.
- List all of the people who were in the room or area when the suspicious mail was recognized. Give this list to local health authorities and law enforcement officials.

VEHICLE BOMB SEARCH

Under the current situation, your vehicle is unlikely to be rigged with a bomb when you are at home in the United States. If you have fear that it might be so rigged, or if the situation changes to the degree that this becomes a concern, see *"Vehicle Bomb Search," page 111*, for suggestions on how to secure your vehicle or to recognize whether it has been rigged with a bomb or otherwise tampered with.

SPECIAL PRECAUTIONS FOR CHILDREN

Child abductions seem to be on the rise in the United States. Motives can include murder, sexual assault, greed (ransom money), or child replacement. Although unlikely in the United States, kidnapping can also be used as a tool to extort money to finance terrorist organizations or as an attempt to force you to assist in a terrorist operation. Special precautions include the following:

- Never leave children alone or unattended. Leave children only with responsible and trustworthy individuals capable of handling emergency situations.
- Instruct children to keep doors and windows locked, and never to allow strangers into the house. Discourage children from answering the door, especially during hours of darkness.
- If possible, locate children's rooms in areas not easily accessible from the outside.
- Instruct children never to leave home without telling their parents. They should travel only in groups and should avoid isolated areas, especially when traveling to and from school. Parents should accompany young children to and from bus stops, where necessary.
- Children should use only approved play areas where recreational activities are supervised by responsible adults and where police protection is readily available.
- Children should refuse automobile rides from

strangers and refuse to accompany strangers anywhere on foot, even if a stranger says, "Your mom [or dad] sent me and said it was okay."

- Inform school authorities never to release children to any person who is not a family member. Instruct children to call home if a stranger comes to pick them up.
- Tell children to refuse gifts from strangers and to avoid providing information to strangers, such as their name and where they live.
- Instruct children to immediately report any strangers who approach them to the nearest person or authority (teacher, police, or known adult).
- Instruct children not to discuss what you do and tell them to inform you if they are questioned about you by anyone.

Make a Kit

If a terrorist incident occurs in the United States, it will most likely be in the form of a WMD attack, not a home invasion or personal assault. In case of such an attack, having emergency supply kits will put the necessary tools at your fingertips. Think of it like having a smoke detector and fire extinguisher in case of a fire. As you consider what to include in your emergency supply kit, be prepared to improvise and use what you have on hand to be self-sufficient for at least three days, maybe longer.

While there are many things that might make you more comfortable, think first about fresh water, food, and clean air. Start now by gathering basic emergency supplies: flashlight, battery-powered radio, extra batteries, first aid kit, utility knife, toilet articles, feminine hygiene products, local map, garbage bags and other sanitation supplies, prescription medicines, and any special items your family may need, including extra cash and identification. Remember to include, and periodically rotate, medications you take every day, such as insulin and heart medicine. Plan to store items in an easy-to-carry bag, such as a shopping bag, backpack, or duffle bag. Consider having two kits. One would contain everything you will need to stay where you are and make it on your own. The other should be a lightweight, smaller version you can take with you if you have to get away.

WATER

You should keep at least a three-day supply of water per person. As a rule of thumb, you will need one gallon of water per person per day for drinking and sanitation.

- Store water tightly in clean, reusable plastic containers; you can purchase bottles in various sizes at your local department store.
- If you live in a warm weather climate, more water will probably be necessary.
- Children, nursing mothers, and sick people usually need more water.

FOOD

Store at least a three-day supply of non-perishable food.

- Select foods that require no refrigeration, preparation, or cooking and little or no water.
- Choose foods your family will eat.
    - Ready-to-eat canned meats, fruits and vegetables
    - Protein or fruit bars
    - Dry cereal or granola
    - Peanut butter
    - Dried fruit
    - Nuts
    - Crackers
    - Canned juices
    - Non-perishable pasteurized milk

- High-energy foods
- Vitamins
- Food for infants
- Comfort and stress foods

- Pack the following for storage and dining:
  - Manual can opener
  - Mess kits, or paper cups, paper plates, and plastic utensils
  - Aluminum foil
  - Plastic storage containers

CLEAN AIR

Many potential terrorist attacks could send tiny microscopic particles into the air. Many of these materials can hurt you only if they get into your body, so think about creating barriers between yourself and any contamination. These should include environmental barriers as well as personal protection.

Nose and Mouth Protection

Be prepared to improvise with what you have on hand to protect your nose, mouth, eyes, and any cuts in your skin. Anything that fits snugly over your nose and mouth, including any dense-weave cotton material, can help filter contaminants in an emergency. Plan to use two to three layers of a cotton t-shirt, handkerchief, or towel. It is very important that most of the air you breathe comes through the mask or cloth, not around it. Do whatever you can to make the best fit possible for children. There are also numerous kinds of face masks readily available in hardware stores that are rated based on how small a particle they can filter in an industrial setting.

Given the different types of attacks that could occur, there is no single solution for masking. For instance, simple cloth face masks can filter some of the airborne "junk" or germs you might breathe into your body, but will probably not protect you from chemical gases. Still, something over your nose and mouth in an emergency is better than nothing. Limiting how much "junk" gets into your body may have an impact on whether or not you get sick or develop disease.

Other Barriers

There are circumstances when staying put and creating a barrier between yourself and potentially contaminated air outside, a process known as "shelter-in-place," is a matter of survival. You will need the following items:

- Heavyweight plastic garbage bags or plastic sheeting
- Duct tape
- Scissors

You can use these materials to tape up windows, doors, and air vents if you need to seal off a room from outside contamination. Consider pre-cutting and labeling them. Anything you can do in advance will save time when it counts.

If there is an incident, use available information to assess the situation. If you see large amounts of debris in the air, or if local authorities say the air is badly contaminated, you can use these things to seal off a room. For more information, see *"Should I Stay or Should I Go?," page 72*, and *"Deciding to Stay or Go," page 178*.

High Efficiency Particulate Air Filtration (HEPA) Filter Fans

Sealing off a room with plastic sheeting and duct tape is better than a simple door for blocking contaminants that may be outside. No seal is perfect, however, and some leakage is likely. Also, you may find yourself in a space that is already contaminated to some degree.

Consider purchasing a portable air purifier, with a High Efficiency Particulate Air Filtration (HEPA) filter, to help remove contaminants from the room where you are sheltering. These highly efficient filters have small sieves that can capture very tiny particles, including some biological agents. Once trapped within a HEPA filter, contaminants cannot get into your body and make you sick. While these filters are excellent at filtering dander, dust, molds, smoke, biological agents, and other contaminants, they will not stop chemical gases.

FIRST AID KIT

In any emergency, you or a family member may be cut or burned, or may suffer other injuries. If you have a basic first aid kit, you will be better prepared to help anyone who is hurt. Remember, many injuries are not life-threatening and do not require immediate medical attention. Knowing how to treat minor injuries can make a difference in an emergency. You should consider taking a first aid class, but simply having the following things can help you stop bleeding, prevent infection, and assist in decontamination.

Basic Necessities

- Two pairs of sterile gloves (the most common kind are latex, but some people are allergic)
- Sterile dressings to stop bleeding

- Cleansing agent/soap and antibiotic towelettes to disinfect
- Antibiotic ointment to prevent infection
- Burn ointment to prevent infection
- Adhesive bandages in a variety of sizes
- Thermometer
- Medicine dropper
- Eye wash solution to flush the eyes or as a general decontaminant
- Prescription medications you take every day, such as insulin, heart medicine, and asthma inhalers
- Prescribed medical supplies, such as glucose and blood-pressure monitoring equipment and supplies
- Scissors
- Tweezers
- Tube of petroleum jelly or other lubricant

Non-Prescription Drugs

- Potassium iodide
  (see *Chapter 4: "Nuclear Blast," page 150*)
- Aspirin or non-aspirin pain reliever
- Anti-diarrhea medication
- Antacid (for upset stomach)
- Syrup of Ipecac (use to induce vomiting, only if advised by the Poison Control Center)

- Laxative
- Activated charcoal (use only if advised by the Poison Control Center)

SPECIAL NEEDS ITEMS AND SUGGESTIONS

Remember the special needs of your family members. Infants, the elderly, and persons with disabilities need the same planning as everyone else, and sometimes a little more, to be prepared for a terrorist attack (or any emergency).

For Babies

- Formula
- Diapers
- Bottles
- Powdered milk
- Medications
- Moist towelettes
- Diaper rash ointment

For Adults

- Ask your doctor about storing prescription medications such as heart medicine, high blood pressure medication, and insulin.

- Contact lenses and supplies
- Extra eyeglasses

Advice for Seniors

- Plan how you will evacuate or signal for help.
- Plan emergency procedures with home health care agencies or workers.
- Tell others where you keep your emergency supplies.
- Teach others how to operate necessary equipment.

Supplies for Seniors

- List of prescription medications, including dosage
- List of allergies, including reactions to medication
- Denture needs
- Extra eyeglasses and hearing-aid batteries
- Extra wheelchair batteries or other special equipment
- A list of the style and serial numbers of medical devices such as pacemakers
- Copies of medical insurance and Medicare cards
- List of doctors and emergency contacts

Advice for People with Disabilities

- Create a support network to help in an emergency.

- Tell these people where you keep your emergency supplies.
- Give one member of your support network a key to your house or apartment.
- Contact your city or county government's emergency information management office. Many local offices keep lists of people with disabilities so they can be located quickly in a sudden emergency.
- Wear medical alert tags or bracelets to help identify your disability.
- If you are dependent on dialysis or other life-sustaining treatment, know the location and availability of more than one facility.
- Show others how to operate your wheelchair.
- Know the size and weight of your wheelchair, in addition to whether or not it is collapsible, in case it has to be transported.

Supplies for People with Disabilities:

- List of prescription medications, including dosage
- List of allergies, including reactions to medication
- Extra eyeglasses and hearing-aid batteries
- Extra wheelchair batteries
- Extra oxygen
- A list of the style and serial number of any medical

devices you use
- Copies of medical insurance and Medicare cards
- List of doctors, relatives, or friends who should be notified if you are hurt

GENERAL SUPPLIES

Water, food, and clean air are necessary to human survival. A first aid kit is essential in case of injury or ongoing medical needs. Following are lists of other basic necessities, from communication devices and bedding to tools and documents.

Basic Supplies

- Cash or traveler's checks, change
- Flashlight and extra batteries
- Battery-powered radio and extra batteries
- First aid kit
- Map of the area for evacuation or for locating shelters
- A whistle to signal for help
- Paper towels
- Moist towelettes

Clothing and Bedding

If you live in a cold weather climate, you must think

about warmth. It is possible that the power will be out and you will not have heat. Rethink your clothing and bedding supplies once a year to account for growing children and other family changes.

Have at least one complete change of warm clothing and shoes per person:

- A jacket or coat
- Long pants
- A long-sleeved shirt
- Sturdy shoes
- A hat and gloves

And don't forget bedding needs:

- A sleeping bag or warm blanket for each person
- A tube tent for every two people

Tools

- Utility knife
- Fire extinguisher: small canister, ABC type
- Pliers
- Compass
- Matches in a waterproof container

- Signal flare
- Paper, pencil
- Shut-off wrench, to turn off household gas and water

Sanitation

- Toilet paper
- Moist towelettes
- Feminine supplies
- Personal hygiene items
- Plastic garbage bags and ties (for personal sanitation)
- Plastic bucket with tight lid
- Disinfectant
- Household chlorine bleach (can be used as a disinfectant, diluted nine parts water to one part bleach, or in an emergency to purify water—16 drops of regular liquid bleach per gallon of water; do not use scented, or color-safe bleach, or bleaches with added cleaners)

Important Documents

- Copies of important family records such as insurance policies, identification, and bank account records in a portable waterproof container.

- Emergency reference material such as a first aid book or a printout of this information

Make a Plan

You should plan for what you will do in an emergency. Be prepared to assess the situation, to use common sense and whatever you have on hand to take care of yourself and your loved ones. Think about the places where your family spends time: Schools, daycare providers, workplaces, neighborhoods, and apartment buildings, like individuals and families, should all have site-specific emergency plans. Ask about their plans. Find out how they will communicate with families during an emergency. If they do not have an emergency plan, consider helping develop one. Consider the community as well. Talk to your neighbors about how you can work together in the event of a crisis. You will be better prepared to safely reunite your family and loved ones during an emergency if you think ahead and communicate with others in advance.

Find out what kinds of disasters, both natural and man-made, are most likely to occur in your area and how you will be notified. Methods of getting your attention vary from community to community. One common method is to broadcast via emergency radio and television broadcasts. You might hear a special siren or get a telephone call, or emergency workers may go door-to-door. Call the closest chapter of the American Red Cross (see *Appendices, page 228*) for emergency information that applies to your community.

Be ready to adapt this information to your personal circumstances and make every effort to follow instructions received from the authorities, whether on the scene or through broadcast media. Above all, stay calm, be patient, and think before you act. With these simple preparations, you can be prepared for the unexpected.

CREATING A FAMILY PLAN

Your family may not be together when disaster strikes, so plan how you will contact one another to review what you will do in different situations.

- Ask a friend or family member to take "roll call": Have each family member call or e-mail that person in the event of an emergency. It may be easier to make a long-distance phone call than to call across town, so an out-of-state contact may be in a better position to communicate among separated family members.

- Be sure every member of your family knows the phone number (or e-mail address) and has coins or a prepaid phone card to call the emergency contact.
- You may have trouble getting through, or the telephone system may be down, but be patient.
- The roll-call taker should record everyone's location (or intended destination if on the move) and note how they can be contacted; if a caller cannot be contacted, the roll-call taker should establish times for that person to call in again, so he or she can be included in family decisions.

NEIGHBORHOODS AND APARTMENT BUILDINGS

A community working together during an emergency makes sense. Sharing plans and communicating in advance is a good strategy.

- Find out if anyone has specialized equipment like a power generator, or expertise such as medical knowledge, that might help in a crisis.
- Decide who will check on elderly or disabled neighbors.
- Make back-up plans for children in case you are unable to return home during an emergency.

- You may be in a high-rise building at the time of an attack. See *Chapter 4: "Escape, Evade, or Confront," page 177*, for what to do in this case.

AT WORK

At your workplace, make sure that there is an emergency-preparedness plan. If your employer does not have such a plan, volunteer to help develop one.

If you are an employer, make sure your workplace has a building evacuation plan that is regularly reviewed and practiced with your employees:

- Take a critical look at your heating, ventilation, and air-conditioning systems to determine if they are secure or if they could feasibly be upgraded to better filter potential contaminants. Be sure you know how to turn them off if you need to.
- Think about what to do if your employees can't go home.
- Plan for how you will communicate with employees' families.
- Make sure you have appropriate supplies on hand (see *"Make a Kit," page 54*).
- For more information, see *"Should I Stay or Should I*

Go? below, and *Chapter 4: "Deciding to Stay or Go," page 178.*

AT SCHOOL AND DAYCARE

If you are a parent or the guardian of an elderly or disabled adult, make sure schools or daycare providers have emergency response plans.

- Ask how they will communicate with families during a crisis.
- Ask if they store adequate food, water, and other basic supplies.
- Find out if they are prepared to "shelter-in-place" if need be, and where they plan to go if they must get away.

IN A MOVING VEHICLE

You may be in a moving vehicle at the time of an attack. See *Chapter 4: "Deciding to Stay or Go," page 178,* for what to do in this case.

SHOULD I STAY OR SHOULD I GO?

Depending on your circumstances and the nature of the

attack, the first important decision is whether you stay put or get away. You should understand and plan for both possibilities. Use common sense and available information to determine whether there is immediate danger. In any emergency, local authorities may or may not immediately be able to provide information on what is happening and what you should do. However, you should watch television, listen to the radio, or check the Internet often for breaking information or official instructions. If you're specifically told to evacuate or seek medical treatment, do so immediately.

This section explains how to prepare for these eventualities. For directions on what to do if a crisis occurs, see *Chapter 4: "Deciding to Stay or Go," page 178*.

Staying Put and "Shelter-in-Place"

Whether you are at home, at work, or elsewhere, there may be situations when it's simply best to stay where you are and avoid any uncertainty outside. In fact, there are some circumstances where staying put and creating a barrier between yourself and potentially contaminated air outside, a process known as "shelter-in-place," is a matter of survival. Plan in advance where you will take shelter in this kind of an emergency. Choose an interior room or one with as few windows and doors as possible. Consider pre-cutting plastic sheeting to seal windows, doors, and air vents. Each piece should be several inches larger than the space you want to cover so that it lies flat against the wall. Label each piece with the location of where it fits.

Getting Away

In case you have to flee your home or your town, plan how you will assemble your family and anticipate where you will go.

- Choose several destinations in different directions so you have options in an emergency.
- Plan places where your family will meet, both within and outside of your immediate neighborhood.
- If you have a car, keep a half tank of gas in it at all times in case you need to evacuate.
- Become familiar with alternate routes and other means of transportation out of your area.
- If you do not have a car, plan how you will leave if you have to.

LEARN HOW AND WHEN TO TURN OFF UTILITIES

In case there is damage to your home or you are instructed to turn off your utilities:

- Locate the electric, gas and water shut-off valves.
- Keep necessary tools near gas and water shut-off valves.
- Teach family members how to turn off utilities.
- If you turn the gas off, a professional must turn it back on. Do not attempt to do this yourself.

PLAN FOR YOUR PETS

For many Americans, animals are an integral part of daily life, even members of the family. Sadly, even those of us with the best of intentions often neglect to plan for their safety in the event of an emergency. Animals—those who live in our houses and in our barns—are often overlooked by both citizens and crisis management planners. Don't do it! Your pets deserve every attention. If they were important enough to care for on a daily level, in normal times, they are important enough to include in your emergency preparedness plans.

Your survival kit should include a list of emergency phone numbers for dealing with pet issues as well as family issues: your veterinarian, local animal shelter, animal care and control, and the American Red Cross.

The following section provides advice on resources to help you provide for animals in a crisis, whether the creatures in your care number one or one hundred. If you need more information, contact your local animal shelter, humane society, or veterinarian.

Shelter and Sustenance

The Humane Society recommends that you never leave your pets behind if you must evacuate your home. Pets generally cannot survive on their own, according to the organization, and if they do, you may not be able to find them when you get back.

This might put you in a bind, however: Most shelters will only admit service animals—guide dogs for the blind, hearing-impaired, or handicapped. Fido and Tabby will most likely be expected to go elsewhere. You might try to find out if there are any pet-friendly shelters being set up in your area. Check with local emergency management officials for more information. You could ask your veterinarian if he or she will accept your pet if an emergency arises; be sure the clinic has a safe room with appropriate food, water, and other supplies, and remember that most kennels require proof of current rabies and distemper vaccinations before they will take in an animal. You might also see if any motels or hotels in communities outside your area will accept pets in an emergency.

If such options do not exist, you will have to find safe

locations in your house or apartment—*never* leave your pet chained outside—where you could leave your pet in an emergency:

- Easily cleaned rooms such as utility closets, bathrooms, or an area in the garage (if you seal the garage)
- Rooms with access to a supply of fresh water
- Rooms with high counters, where animals can go in case of flooding or other floor hazards
- Separate locations for different animals—don't put your dogs with your cats, or your cats with your birds; even if they normally get along, the anxiety of an emergency situation can cause pets to act irrationally
- Do not use rooms that might present pet perils such as windows, hanging plants, or pictures in large frames

Remember these simple precautions as well:

- Leave a list outside your home stating what animals are inside and any special needs they may have
- Include a telephone number so that you or someone else who knows about the animals can be contacted by emergency personnel, if necessary; include your veterinarian's name and number

- Large food and water dispensers, especially for birds
- Two- or three-day supply of dry food for each animal, even if not their usual food; do not moisten it, for it can turn sour or rancid
- For water needs, open a faucet slightly, if possible, and let water drip into a large bowl or bucket; large dogs can drink from a tub
- Leave them with their usual bedding and favorite toys; familiar belongings will keep them in a better mood
- If you have a bird, make sure that it is caged and the cage is covered by a thin cloth or sheet to provide security and filtered light

Transport

If you know you are going to a place where your pets will be welcome, or if you're taking your pet to the vet, you will need a pet carrier. Look for one that's large enough so that your pet can stand up and turn around inside. Then train the animal so that it is comfortable with the carrier (methods include feeding it in the carrier or placing a favorite toy or blanket inside).

Veterinary and Safety Needs

Your animals' medical needs should be as well-attended to as their physical safety. Consult your veterinarian as necessary.

- Know what you should do if your pet is on medication or a special diet
- Be sure to have extra medication on hand
- Be sure that all shots are current
- Know the location of all veterinary records
- Ensure that all collars fit and include current license and rabies tags, as well as identification tags that have your name, address, and phone number; include a tag with the address and phone number of your evacuation site
- If your canine companion normally wears a chain-link "choker," get a leather or nylon collar in case you have to leave him alone for several days

Pet Survival Kit

Consider creating a pet survival kit; this kit can be taken along if you take your animals with you when you evacuate, or it can be taken with them to their new home. Include the following:

- Pet food
- Bottled water

- Medications
- Veterinary records
- Kitty litter/pan
- Can opener
- Food dishes
- First aid kit
- Extra dry food, stored in sturdy containers

After the Emergency

When you first return home—for at least the first few days—your pets may be a bit "off." Animals that are usually quiet and friendly may become aggressive or defensive; familiar landmarks and scents may have changed, and your pet may become confused or lost. You will need to ease them back in to their familiar routine:

- Watch them closely
- Always maintain close contact
- Leash your pets, especially dogs, when they go outside; if you leave them outside, leave them in a fenced yard with access to shelter and water

Livestock

When you're planning for your pets, don't forget other

animals you may own. Your cows and chickens, if you have them, need just as much care as your cats and dogs.

- If possible, you should evacuate your livestock
- You should have routes prepared (and mapped out), and you should always have back-up routes
- Livestock shelters should be fully equipped with food, water, and veterinary care; if your shelters don't have all of these things, they should be readily available
- Vehicles for transporting your livestock should be readily available, along with experienced handlers and drivers; animals should be habituated to these vehicles in advance

Abroad

In the current global situation, Americans are at greatest risk when traveling abroad, especially when traveling to unstable countries or regions where the government is unpopular or in flux. Again, your best policy is to be informed, to be careful, and to plan ahead.

BEFORE YOU GO

As soon as you know that you're going to be traveling

outside the United States, you should learn as much as you can about your destination: the culture, language, local customs, and history of terrorism and criminal activity.

To communicate and to get around:

- Learn common phrases and greetings.
- Learn how to ask for assistance or help in the local language, including phrases such as "I need a policeman" and "I need a doctor."

To learn about general safety in the area:

- Consult U.S. State Department consular information sheets, public service announcements, or travel warnings via the internet. If possible, get detailed information on the cities you plan to visit: any threats, the safest routes to use, areas to avoid, and anything else pertaining to your safety.
- Learn about the area through reading newspapers, magazines, and books, and consulting with travel agents or tourist offices.
- Discuss the region with people who currently live or have lived there.

Before you decide on your destination and when you consider how best to protect yourself once you're there, ask yourself the following questions:

- Are terrorist groups active in the area?
- Are terrorist groups organizing or reorganizing?
- What are the local populace's attitudes toward the terrorist groups?
- What are the local populace's attitudes toward Americans?
- Does the respective foreign government support, condone, or condemn the terrorist activity?
- What is the potential for violence?
- What are the terrorists' methods of operation? (Generally, when a terrorist group is successful with a certain method of operation, it is re-used by the group or it is used by other terrorist groups. However, just because a terrorist group has not used a specific tactic in the past does not mean they won't develop new tactics or adopt similar tactics used by other terrorist groups.)

GETTING THERE

Air travel, particularly through high-risk airports or

countries, poses security problems different from those of ground transportation. Here, too, simple precautions can reduce the hazards of a terrorist assault.

Making Travel Arrangements

- Avoid countries, airports, or airlines that are known to be high-risk or are currently targets of terrorist organizations.
- Direct flights are best; if you must make airline changes, use foreign flag airlines and/or indirect routings to avoid high-risk airports. Choose flights that will route you through an airport with a history of good security measures.
- Buy your ticket at a travel agency that offers you seat selection and gives you a boarding pass when you buy your ticket. Ask for a window seat near the center of the aircraft. This puts you farther away from hijackers' movements up and down the aisle; terrorists generally select passengers for abuse that are sitting in more easily accessible aisle seats.
- Rear seats also offer more protection since they are farther from the center of hostile action which is often near the cockpit.
- Seats at or near an emergency exit may provide greater

opportunity for escape.

- Avoid seats in first class.

Before You Leave for the Airport

- Be sure to bring proper identification to show airline and immigration officials. You must have a passport to travel overseas.
- Inform someone of your destination and get in the habit of checking in with them before you depart and after you reach your destination. This could provide authorities with a starting point if you "disappear."
- Make a copy of your passport, ID card, and any other official papers. Place these in different pieces of luggage. If lost or stolen, these items can be replaced at a U.S. Embassy or Consulate.
- Learn the names and phone numbers of persons to contact at your destination, including emergency numbers.

At the Airport

- Arrive early. Don't loiter near the ticket counter, luggage check-in, or security area. Go as quickly as possible to the boarding area.
- Use the shops, restaurants, and lounges in the security area, not those in the main terminal.

- Don't let your carry-on luggage out of your sight, and don't agree to "watch" someone else's luggage.
- Keep your eyes open for any suspicious activity, such as an individual who gets up and leaves behind bags or a pack.
- Be aware of unattended baggage anywhere in the terminal.
- Look for nervous passengers who maintain eye contact with others from a distance. Observe what people are carrying. Note behavior not consistent with that of others in the area.
- Be extremely observant of personal carry-on luggage. Thefts of briefcases designed for laptop computers are increasing at airports worldwide. Likewise, luggage not properly guarded provides an opportunity for a terrorist to place an unwanted object or device in your carry-on bag. As much as possible, do not pack anything you cannot afford to lose.
- If you see something suspicious, get out of the area quickly and report it to airport security officials!
- When you have a long layover (several hours), stay within the restricted or boarding areas of the airport, or leave the airport if possible or practical.
- No matter where you are in the terminal, identify objects suitable for cover in the event of an attack. Pillars, trash cans, luggage, large planters, counters,

and furniture can provide some protection.

- Sit with your back against a wall, facing the crowd, so that you have greater awareness of your surroundings.
- Avoid secluded areas that provide concealment for attackers.
- Observe the baggage-claim area from a distance. Do not retrieve your bags until the crowd clears. Proceed to the customs lines at the edge of the crowd.

Actions if Attacked in an Airport

- Dive for cover. Do not run. Running increases the probability of shrapnel hitting vital organs or the head.
- If you must move, crawl on your belly or roll. Stay low to the ground, using available cover.
- If you see grenades, seek immediate cover, lay flat on the floor, feet and knees tightly together with soles toward the grenade. In this position, your shoes, feet, and legs protect the rest of your body. Shrapnel will rise in a cone from the point of detonation, passing over your body. Place arms and elbows next to your ribcage to protect your lungs, heart, and chest. Cover your ears and head with your hands to protect neck, arteries, ears, and skull.

- Responding security personnel will not be able to distinguish you from attackers. Do not attempt to assist them in any way. Lie still until told to get up.

On the Plane

- Count the number of seats to the closest emergency exit so that you will be able to find your way out in case the lights go out or the compartment fills with smoke.
- On a foreign carrier, avoid speaking English as much as possible.

Actions if Hijacked

- Remain calm, be polite, and cooperate with your captors.
- Be aware that all hijackers may not reveal themselves at the same time. A lone hijacker may be used to draw out security personnel for neutralization by other hijackers.
- Don't draw attention to yourself with sudden body movements, remarks, or hostile looks.
- Prepare yourself for possible verbal and physical abuse, as well as lack of food, drink, and sanitary conditions.
- If permitted, read, sleep, or write to occupy your time.
- Discreetly observe your captors and memorize their physical descriptions. Include voice patterns and language distinctions, as well as clothing and unique

physical characteristics.

- Cooperate with any rescue attempt. Lie on the floor until told to rise.

WHEN YOU ARRIVE

Upon arrival, there are certain habits and safety measures that you should keep in mind.

- Remain alert; travel in groups or pairs in well-lighted, busy areas.
- Establish alternate routes from each starting place to each destination.
- Make sure at least one person you work with and someone in your family are aware of these routes and the approximate time it takes you to travel these routes.
- Keep travel arrangements confidential as much as possible.
- Register with the U.S. Embassy upon arrival; you can do this in person or over the phone. Carry a card that has the location and phone number of the U.S. Embassy and Consulates, as well as U.S. military installations, in the area. These are vital safe havens during emergencies.
- Avoid using public transportation. Buses and trains are

preferred to taxis. If you must travel in a taxi, specify the route you want the taxi driver to take and ensure that the license or identification photo matches the driver.

- Know how to use public phones and carry enough change (in the local currency) to make a phone call. In many countries, calling cards are an option.
- Know emergency numbers and how to use the local telephone system.

Family Members

Of course, knowledge of precautions and safety habits should not be limited to the family leader or organizer of the trip. Everyone in the group should practice basic precautions for their personal security. Familiarize your family or traveling companions with the local terrorist threat and regularly review your protective measures and techniques. Ensure that everyone in the group knows what to do in an emergency.

Following are important precautions for every traveler:

- Know the threat risk for the area.
- Know where you are at all times. A simple orientation to the area could prevent travelers from straying into

dangerous areas.

- If staying in a house, keep the doors and windows locked whenever you leave. Exercise caution upon return. Set up simple signals to alert family members or associates if there is danger. (For detailed information on safety points for those residing long-term in a foreign country, see *"Staying in a Foreign Country," page 101.*)
- Develop and practice emergency procedures for use in the home, such as:
  - Evacuation due to fire
  - Intruders in the residence upon arriving home
  - Intruders breaking into the house
- Know the location and phone numbers of the U.S. Embassy and nearest Consulate, neighbors, and all emergency services such as police, fire department, and medical services, and other safe locations for refuge or assistance.
- Carry small cards with emergency phrases in the respective foreign language, and post these phrases by the telephone.
- In preparation for emergencies, maintain survival items (for detailed suggestions, see *"Make a Kit," page 54*).
- Take an ample supply of medications that family

members use. Also, keep a copy of the prescription and a statement from a physician, and know the generic name of the medication so you can reorder it abroad.

- Carry a card stating blood type and allergies to particular medications. The card should be multilingual, with information provided in English and in any language or languages commonly used in the host nation.
- Keep eyeglass prescriptions on hand.
- Always carry identification documents.

VISIBILITY

"Visibility" is the U.S. military term for how noticeable you are, how much you stand out when in a foreign country. The basic rules of self-protection when living or traveling abroad are as follows: Be alert to your surroundings; know and respect local customs and laws; be unpredictable by varying the days and times of your activities and by varying routes you usually travel; don't call undue attention to yourself.

Keep a Low Profile. Your dress, conduct, and mannerisms should not attract attention. Make an effort to blend into the local environment. Avoid publicity and don't go out in large groups. Stay away from civil disturbances and demonstrations.

Be Unpredictable. You are the most vulnerable and predictable in the morning as you enter or leave your quarters, your place of work, or your vehicle. Vary your route to and from work and the time you leave and return home. Vary your dress. Don't exercise at the same time and place each day, and never do so alone, on deserted streets, or on country roads. Let people close to you know where you are going, what you'll be doing, and when you plan to be back.

Be Alert. Watch for anything suspicious or out of place. Don't give personal information over the telephone. If you think you are being followed, go to a pre-selected secure area. Immediately report the incident to local law enforcement agencies and to the nearest Embassy or Consulate.

Anyone who is highly visible is a potential high-risk victim. Victims can be targeted for being an American, a very important person (VIP) or a person associated with VIPs, or a target of opportunity.

Identified as an American

One way to protect yourself from becoming a target is to avoid saying, doing, wearing, using, displaying, or driving anything that readily identifies you as an American. Even if the local populace does not see Americans on a daily basis, global commerce and communications provide them with access to magazines, movies, television shows, and web sites that portray American lifestyles. The following paragraphs identify and suggest ways to change common indicators that easily identify Americans overseas.

Dress. Blend in with what the local populace or local tourist element wears. Flashy or trendy clothing can attract unwanted attention. Clothes should not clearly identify you as an American; beware of cowboy boots, American logo T-shirts, clothes bearing American sports teams, and expensive athletic shoes, for instance.

Speech. Although American dialect is hard to avoid, even if you speak the native language, avoid using American slang.

Customs and Habits. Even if you physically blend in with the local populace, your customs and habits can identify you as an American. If possible, you should adopt local customs and habits.

Personal Behavior. Some Americans have the tendency to be loud and obnoxious in the presence of the local populace. Another common mistake that Americans can make is to unnecessarily boast about American culture, wealth, technology, military power, and other "strengths" in the presence of foreign nationals. Strive to blend in as much as possible, and to not draw attention to yourself. Keep a low profile, especially in a public environment or with the local media.

Controversial Materials. Avoid carrying potentially controversial materials such as gun magazines, military publications, religious books, pornography, or magazines that can offend the local populace.

Nationality Indicators. U.S. flags, decals, patches or logos easily identify you as an American. Avoid displaying them on your vehicles, or clothes, in front of your home, or at your place of employment.

Currency. Exchange U.S. dollars into the local currency before arriving overseas. Use local currency and avoid carrying large amounts of money.

Identified as Someone of Importance

Many people, including terrorists, equate certain lifestyles with prominence. They believe that a prominent lifestyle is indicative of a person's importance to his or her company or government. Americans, in particular, are often treated by host governments as VIPs out of respect. Whenever possible, avoid being treated as a VIP.

Avoid using your title or position when introducing yourself or signing your name. Strive to maintain a low profile and to blend in with the local populace. The issues identified in the following paragraphs give the impression of importance and therefore should be avoided.

Expensive Cars. People may think anyone who drives an expensive car is important. Avoid driving expensive vehicles. Drive the type of vehicle that is common to the area in which you are located.

Bodyguards. If you do not need bodyguards, do not use them. If you must have bodyguards, keep them to a minimum and ensure that they blend in with the other personnel around you. They should not be obvious. Do a background check on each potential bodyguard, and ensure that he or she is well-trained.

Chauffeurs. Many people may believe that anyone who has a driver is a VIP. Therefore, do your own driving whenever possible. Typically, VIPs with drivers sit in the rear right seat. Therefore, if you choose to have (or need to have) a driver, sit up front with him or her and occasionally rotate your seat position within the vehicle. You should also

- Ensure that your driver is trained not to panic or freeze in a high-pressure situation.
- Develop an all-clear or distress signal (e.g., a hat or cigarette pack on the dash) to allow the driver to warn you of a problem prior to your approaching the vehicle.
- Have the driver open the door for you.
- Avoid giving your itinerary to your driver. All a driver needs to know is when and where to be. If possible, tell your driver your destination only after the car has been started.

Briefcases. In some countries, people think anyone carrying a briefcase is important. If possible, avoid carrying a briefcase unless it is the norm for the area. If the local populace uses backpacks, then you should also use a backpack.

Parking. VIPs warrant their own parking spots, usually very close to their offices. This draws attention. You should avoid using a designated parking space; instead, park in an unmarked parking space and rotate where you park your vehicle.

Domestic Employees. In many foreign countries, domestic employees—such as maids, cooks, private guards, gardeners, and drivers—are very affordable. However, domestic help can provide terrorists with critical access to you and your family. If you are considering employing domestic help, ask for letters of reference and obtain a background check through the embassy, if possible. Other precautions include the following:

- Avoid live-in domestic help. If such employees must have access to keys, never let them remove the keys from the house.
- Domestic employees should not allow anyone (including persons in police uniforms) to enter the house without permission from the family.
- Avoid providing transportation to and from work for any domestic employees. Pay for a taxi or bus fare.
- If a domestic employee calls in sick, do not accept the temporary services of a relative ("cousin" or "sister").
- Have domestic employees report potential terrorist surveillance of your residence and watch for anyone loitering in the area or repeatedly driving or walking by.
- Pay domestic help well and give cash rewards for following your security rules.
- Take special care never to discuss sensitive topics or detailed travel plans in the presence of domestic employees. Terrorists have successfully drawn this information from such workers in the past.

- Instruct them which phone or other means of communication to use in an emergency.
- Discuss duties in friendly, firm manner.
- Give presents or gratuities according to local customs.

Identified as a Target of Opportunity

In June 1985, four U.S. Marine guards of the U.S. Embassy in San Salvador became targets of opportunity for the Faribundo Marti Para la Liberacion Nacional (FMLN) terrorist organization. These Marines were sitting outside of a very popular café in San Salvador when they were gunned down for being symbols of the United States. When overseas, remember that you are a visual symbol of an American presence and of our values, prestige, and power. The longer you remain overseas, the more comfortable you may become. The more comfortable you become, the less you may think of yourself as a potential target. While overseas, never allow yourself to become complacent. Safeguard information concerning yourself, your home, your job, and your family. The more intelligence a terrorist can collect on you, the greater his chance of success. Terrorists gather their information from a variety of sources:

- Various Internet sources.

- Bills of lading can provide names of people moving into and out of an area.
- Immigration records provide names of people, dates of birth, and nationalities.
- Telephone directories provide an individual's name, address, and phone number. If you must list your phone number in the telephone directory, request that only your name and number be included, not your address.
- Discarded mail or official correspondence can be used to identify an individual, the sender, and the place from which the correspondence was sent. Destroy any mail or official correspondence no longer needed and remove address labels from magazines.
- Some companies and stores still use credit cards receipts that feature carbon copies. These carbons provide an individual's name and account number. Use the currency of the country you are visiting or working in. If you must use a credit card, request the carbon as well as your customer receipt.
- Checks can provide an individual's name, address, phone number, and social security number. Have only minimal information printed on the front of your checks.
- Nameplates make it easy to find an individual in an office environment; avoid their use, if possible.

- Receipts from hotels, laundries, and other businesses often identify an individual by name and by room number. Consider using a nickname or an assumed name.
- Remove all destination and baggage-claim tags from luggage, as well as stickers, decals, and other markings that reveal that the luggage has been through U.S. Customs.
- Be aware of all the documentation that contains informationabout you and your family. Before putting any such documentation into the trash, shred or destroy it; it could be used by terrorists as a source of information.

STAYING IN A FOREIGN COUNTRY

As noted previously, you are most at risk from terrorist attacks when you are traveling or living abroad. In many countries, Americans are hated or even feared; all over the world, Americans are often targets of terrorism and crime simply because they are Americans. This section offers numerous suggestions for how to prevent or avoid dangerous situations and what to do in the case of an attack or other attempt against your freedom or your life.

Safeguards while Staying in Hotels

If you are visiting a foreign country for a short vacation, you will most likely stay in a hotel, unless you have friends who live in that country. Following are some suggestions for improving security of your room and your person.

- Request another room if one has been reserved for you.
- Do not give your room number to strangers.
- Avoid street-level rooms. Ask for a room between the second floor and the eighth floor. This puts you high enough to prevent easy access from the outside and low enough for local fire equipment to reach.
- Before exiting from an elevator or your room, check for objects that seem out of place or for strangers who seem to be loitering.
- Answer the hotel phone with "Hello," not your name.
- Never answer hotel paging. If you are expecting someone, go to the lobby, but don't go to the desk and identify yourself; check to see if the caller is the person you are waiting for.
- Keep your room key on you at all times. Don't leave a copy of your room key on your key chain for the parking attendants.
- Be careful answering the door. Check to see who it is

through the peephole or side window. Also, arrange knock signals with your traveling companions.

- Watch for anyone loitering in halls, lobbies, or public areas or for anyone carrying objects that could be used as a weapon.
- Vary your arrival and departure times.
- Vary how you enter and exit the building; e.g., use a hotel's entrance as well as its elevators and stairwells.
- Know where emergency exits and fire extinguishers are located.
- Avoid frequent exposure on windows and balconies. Keep your room draperies closed.
- Conduct business in your room, not in the lobby or hallways.
- Inspect your room thoroughly upon entering. Keep your room and personal effects neat and orderly. This practice helps you recognize tampering or strange or out-of-place objects.
- Place a piece of tape on the door crack or a string in the doorjamb. If it has moved while you were out, you will know that someone has entered your room during your absence.
- Lock the door and use the chain.
- Place the DO NOT DISTURB sign on the door.
- Avoid maid service.

- Never admit a stranger to your room.
- Consider purchasing a portable door alarm; this will awaken you if someone attempts to enter while you are sleeping.
- Place a large screw into the space between the door and the door frame; this will delay anyone's entry into the room.
- Leave lights, television, or radio on when you are out of the room to give the appearance that someone is still there.
- Find out if the hotel has security guards; if so, determine how many, their hours of duty, their equipment, their expertise, and how to locate them by phone and in person.
- Do not discuss travel plans over hotel phones. The lines could be "bugged."
- Do not take the first taxi in line when leaving your hotel, and don't allow strangers to direct you to a specific cab.

Residential Security

If you take up residence in another country, whether for a long vacation or a long-term work situation, there are certain precautions you should take or habits you should build, and certain features your residence should have.

GENERAL PRECAUTIONS

- Develop friendly relations with your neighbors.
- Don't draw attention to yourself.

- Avoid frequent exposure on balconies and near windows.
- Be alert to public works crews and other foreign nationals requesting access to residence; check their identities through a peephole before allowing entry.
- Report all suspicious activity to local law enforcement.

EXTERIOR GROUNDS

- Do not put your name on the outside of your residence or mailbox.
- Have good lighting.
- Control vegetation to eliminate hiding places.
- Make sure you have a clear view of approaches.
- Have more than one access road.
- Establish off-street parking.
- If necessary, build a high perimeter wall or fence (6 to 8 feet is a good height).

ENTRANCES AND EXITS

- Solid doors with deadbolt locks
- One-way peepholes in door
- Bars and locks on skylights
- Metal grating on glass doors and ground floor windows, with interior release mechanisms that are not reachable from outside

INTERIOR FEATURES

- Alarms and intercom systems
- Fire extinguishers
- Medical and first aid equipment

OUTSIDE YOUR HOME AWAY FROM HOME

When you are traveling within a foreign country or city, you must be as careful as you are when you're in your hotel or residence. Criminal and terrorist acts against individuals usually occur outside the home and after the victim's habits have been established. Your most predictable habit is the route of travel from home to duty station or to commonly frequented local facilities. You must be careful in how you travel, what you do, and, if you have your own car, how you maintain it and behave while driving.

General

- Travel in small groups as much as possible. Avoid high-risk areas such as demonstrations, and vary movements so as not to be predictable.
- Try to be inconspicuous when using public transportation and facilities. Dress, conduct, and mannerisms should not attract attention.

- Do not be curious about spontaneous gatherings or demonstrations. Avoid them.
- Stay away from known trouble spots or disreputable places; visit only reputable establishments, but don't frequent the same locations all the time (in particular, known, U.S.-associated locales).

Auto Maintenance

- Keep vehicle in good repair.
- Always keep gas tank at least half-full.
- Ensure that tires have sufficient tread.
- Keep safety equipment (e.g., cellular phone, fire extinguisher) inside your vehicle in good working order. Consider carrying a first aid kit and an emergency survival kit (see *"Make a Kit," page 54*).

Parking Your Car

- Always lock your car.
- Park your car for easy escape (pointed outwards).
- Try not to leave your car on the street overnight. If you must do so, park in well-lighted areas.
- Never get out without checking for suspicious persons. If in doubt, drive away.
- Leave only the ignition key with parking attendant.

- Don't leave garage doors open or unlocked.
- Use a remote garage door opener if available. Enter and exit your car in the security of the closed garage.
- Lock your car and garage when you park overnight. Alternate use of parking garages if possible.

On the Road

- Walk to your car with keys in hand, ready to use.
- Before leaving buildings to get into your vehicle, check the surrounding area to determine if anything of a suspicious nature exists. Display the same wariness before exiting your vehicle.
- Prior to getting into a vehicle, check it for bombs (see *"Vehicle Bomb Search," page 111*).
- Start your car immediately after conducting your vehicle bomb search. Do this before you adjust your seat or mirrors. You should be prepared for rapid escape if necessary.
- If possible, vary times and routes to work and home.
- Avoid late-night travel.
- Travel with companions.
- Know the locations of dangerous areas in the city and and avoid them.
- Avoid isolated roads or dark alleys when possible.
- Travel only on busy, well-traveled thoroughfares,

especially routes that allow speeds over 25 mph. Most attacks occur in stop-and-go traffic. Avoid one-way streets and other choke points such as bridges, traffic circles, and narrow alleyways. Avoid isolated secondary roads.

- Enter and exit your vehicle at busy locations.
- If possible, use different building entrances and exits.
- Habitually ride with seatbelts buckled, doors locked, and windows closed.
- Never pick up hitchhikers.
- In an emergency, drive on flat tires until reaching a well-lighted, well-traveled area or safe haven.
- Avoid driving close behind other vehicles or in any situation where you can get boxed in or forced to a curb. Maintain a minimum 8-foot interval between you and the vehicle in front of you; avoid the inner lanes. Be alert while driving or riding. Have an evasive plan ready; sometimes, making a simple U-turn is enough to get you out of danger.
- Keep at least one-half car length of empty space in front of your vehicle when stopped at traffic signals and stop signs. This gives you room to escape in a kidnapping or armed attack/assassination attempt.
- Know how to react if you are being followed; see *"Detecting Surveillance," page 125*).

- In the event of mechanical failure, set out warning triangles/flares, raise the hood, activate emergency flashers, and stay inside the vehicle. If someone stops to offer assistance, ask them to notify the police or road service. If you feel unsure of the situation, don't get out of the car until the police or road service arrives. If you feel threatened by strangers, stay in the car with the doors locked. Use your vehicle's horn to attract attention.
- Recognize events that signal the start of an attack. When one of these events occurs, start mentally preparing a course of action in case an attack develops. These events may include, but are not limited to:
  - Cyclist falling in front of your car
  - Flagman or workman stopping your car
  - Unusual or false police or government checkpoint
  - Disabled vehicle/accident victims on the road
  - Unusual detours
  - An accident in which your car is struck
  - Cars or pedestrian traffic that box you in
  - Sudden activity or gunfire
- Know what to do if under attack in a vehicle:
  - Without subjecting yourself, passengers, or pedestrians to harm, draw attention to your car by sounding the horn.

- Put another vehicle between you and your pursuer.
- Execute immediate turn and escape; jump the curb at a 45-degree angle, 35 mph maximum.
- Ram blocking vehicle if necessary.
- Go to closest safe haven.
- Report incident to police.

Vehicle Bomb Search

A large number of terrorist attacks take place in or around a vehicle, typically involving some sort of explosive device. This is because bombs are relatively easy to make and equally easy to plant on exposed and unattended vehicles. You need to learn how to search a vehicle for tampering and to recognize danger signs. By routinely inspecting your vehicle, you give the impression of being a hard target.

PREVENTION

There are certain procedures that may help prevent you from becoming a victim of a vehicle bombing:

- Check your vehicle at irregular times to prevent establishing a pattern.
- Be suspicious and aware of what is going on around you.
- Lock your vehicle and park in secured areas whenever

possible to limit easy access.

- Allow a fine coat of dust to remain on the vehicle surface or apply talcum powder.
- Secure transparent tape to vehicle doors, trunk, and hood to help detect tampering.
- Install two bolts in an X pattern over the open end of the exhaust pipe.
- Install a locking gas cap and a mesh strainer in the mouth of the filler tube.
- Get out of the car to wait for passengers.

EXTERIOR SEARCH

Unless your vehicle has been under twenty-four -hour guard, there is danger of it having been rigged with a bomb. The first, and easiest, check to perform is the exterior search.

You must use extreme caution while conducting this search. You must know your vehicle inside and out so that you can quickly recognize something that is wrong. If possible, a search should be conducted in pairs. If you notice that you are being observed while conducting the search, gently close the hood, trunk, or door (if it is open) and walk away from the vehicle. If you find a bomb, or something that looks like a bomb, do not touch it. Immediately contact local law enforcement or your local embassy, so that an explosive ordnance disposal unit can be dispatched.

An exterior search is conducted as follows:

- Search the area around the vehicle. Look for areas where an improvised explosive device may be placed or concealed; such areas include, but are not limited to, bushes, shrubs, trees, trash cans, and mailboxes. An explosion close to a vehicle can produce the same devastating effects as if the bomb was placed in the vehicle.
- Examine the exterior surfaces of the vehicle. Look for signs of tampering such as wires hanging down or doors, hood, or trunk left ajar. Does anything seem to have changed since you left the vehicle?
- Examine the film of dust or talcum powder. Is it undisturbed? Has another layer of dust appeared?
- Examine the transparent tape: Has it been removed? Is it broken?
- Examine the hood or trunk lock (look, but do not lift). Has either been jimmied?
- Examine the vehicle for other signs of forced entry, including broken windows, scratched paint, and bent or damaged metal.
- Open the interior compartments just a little, enough

to gently run your fingers around the opening to feel for a trip wire.

- If a trip wire is not found, you can open the compartment gradually, examining the hinges for pressure or tension release initiators.
- Look closely for any bits of tape or wire lying in or around the vehicle.
- Examine the ground for any unusual marks or signs of digging.
- Remove the gas cap and look inside.
- Check in and around the exhaust pipe.
- Check the undercarriage. If you can, use a long-handled mirror to help in your search.
- Examine each of the wheel wells and the areas behind the bumpers.
- Examine everywhere: steps, door handles, exterior mirrors, etc.

INTERIOR SEARCH

Once you have finished your exterior search, it is time to move on to the interior. Again, proceed with extreme caution. Always look inside before you move inside. You must avoid touching anything in the interior of the vehicle until it has been searched, and you should never rest your hand on the seat. If you find a bomb, or something that looks like a bomb, do not touch it. Immediately contact local law enforcement or your local embassy, so that an explosive ordnance disposal unit can be dispatched.

An interior search is conducted as follows:

- Look through the windows. Do you see anything out of place? Has anything been moved? Has anything been added, for instance, a package or briefcase that does not belong there? Do you see tapes or wires hanging down?
- Unlock a door, open it very slowly, and to only a quarter of an inch. Look around the door edges for trip wires. If the door looks free of trip wires, open the door gradually, examining the hinges for pressure or tension release initiators. If anything looks suspicious, close the door gently.
- Look at the carpet or floor mats for any suspicious bulges. Look as far as you can under the seat, around the seat, and behind the seat without entering the vehicle.
- Look around and behind all the other seats.
- Slip into the seat and check the ashtray, adjustable headrest, and seat belt.

- Examine the right rear passenger seat.
- Check the glove compartment.
- Look under the dash, checking especially for strange tapes and wires.
- Use a flashlight to check the air-conditioning ducts and other vehicle cavities.
- Examine the sun visors and rear-view mirror for signs of tampering.

ENGINE AND TRUNK SEARCH

Once the interior search has been completed, exit the vehicle and open the engine hood and trunk. Open the hood or the trunk only a quarter of an inch at first and very gently feel for wires along the length of the hood or the trunk.

Engine and trunk searches are conducted as follows:

Engine

- Raise the hood and make a thorough search of the engine compartment and fire wall.
- Look for any strange or new-looking wires attached to the battery, clutch, coil, accelerator, or any power-operated equipment.

- Check engine cavities for anything that looks like it does not belong there and for anything out of place.
- Open the air filter and look inside. Pay special attention to the spark plug wires, the distributor, the ignition area, and the exhaust manifold.

Trunk

- Raise the trunk lid and make a thorough search.
- Check the items inside. Is anything rearranged? Is anything new?
- Check the spare tire to ensure that it is filled with air.

FINAL CHECK BEFORE STARTING THE VEHICLE

Once you have inspected the exterior and interior of the vehicle, the trunk, and the engine, you can get into the driver's seat and check the dashboard. You should look at the turn signals and lights; if nothing is unusual, then turn them on. You also need to check and test the wipers, washer, radio, and horn. Once you feel that the vehicle is safe, you can start it up. Let the vehicle run for about two minutes before you proceed to your destination.

VEHICLE BOMB SEARCH

Following are some basic guidelines for conducting a bomb search of your automobile. Remember, to do a thorough inspection, you must follow the complete directions beginning on page 111. *The steps illustrated here are only highlights. Be very careful: follow* all *directions.*

[1] The first rule in protecting yourself from becoming the victim of a bomb in your own vehicle is to be always suspicious and ever alert to what is going on around you. It is also very important, especially as an American abroad, to check your vehicle at irregular times; this prevents any would-be attackers from establishing a pattern, and makes them less likely to attack you in the first place—people who are alert to their surroundings and who avoid predictable habits make poor targets.

[2] One of the easiest places to attempt sabotage of a vehicle is the exhaust system; it is very easy for an attacker to install a pipe bomb or other device in the main exhaust pipe. To prevent such access, install two bolts in an X pattern over the open end of the exhaust pipe. Another easy access point for bombers is the gas filler tube; you should install a locking gas cap and a mesh strainer in the mouth of the filler tube.

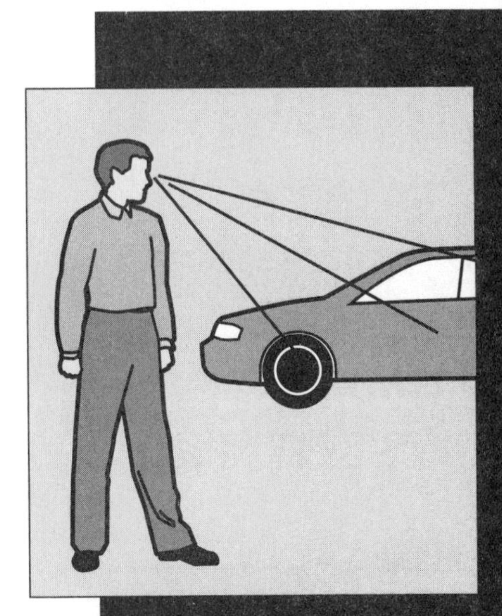

[3] Unless your vehicle is under constant guard, there is danger of it being rigged with a bomb. The very first step in ensuring that it has not been so rigged is the exterior search. You must know your vehicle inside and out so that you can quickly recognize anything unusual. Signs of tampering may include wires hanging down or doors, hood, or trunk left ajar. Ask yourself, Does anything seem to have changed since you left the vehicle? If you find a bomb, or something that looks like a bomb, do not try to deal with it yourself. Instead, get in touch with local law enforcement or your local embassy or consulate, so that experts can be dispatched to the scene.

[4] Part of any thorough exterior search is an organized and comprehensive examination of the undercarriage, wheel wells, and tires of your vehicle. A long-handled mirror is a great tool for such an examination; it allows you to look closely at all those areas without getting near them. Of course, you must be careful to avoid any suspect wires that are hanging down or any levers or trigger devices. So before you use the mirror, look closely for unusual wires and for any bits of tape or wire lying in or around the vehicle, and examine the ground for any unusual marks or signs of digging.

[5] Once you've searched the exterior and interior of your vehicle, you need to search the engine (and the trunk). Lift the hood and thoroughly examine the engine compartment and fire wall: Are there any strange or new-looking wires attached to the battery, clutch, coil, accelerator, or any power-operated equipment? Check engine cavities for anything that does not seem to belong. Open the air filter and look inside. Pay special attention to the spark plug wires, the distributor, the ignition area, and the exhaust manifold.

[6] The air filter is an excellent hiding place for small, improvised explosive devices—it's easy to get to and easy to open; all an attacker has to do is unscrew the wing nut. When you open your air filter, there should be nothing inside except the filter itself. If anything looks unusual, call the authorities immediately. Do not try to remove or defuse an explosive on your own; this is a recipe for disaster.

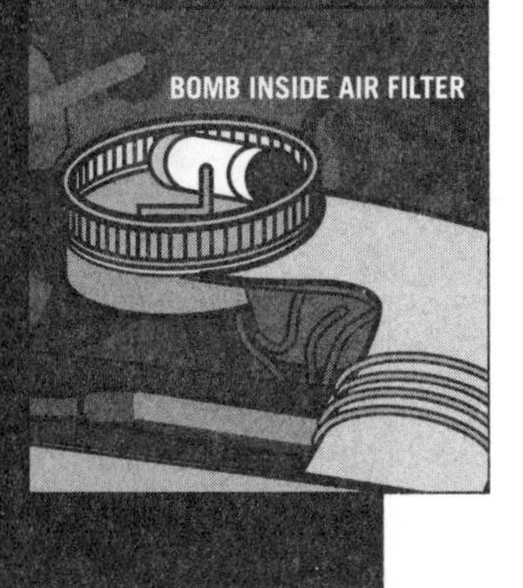

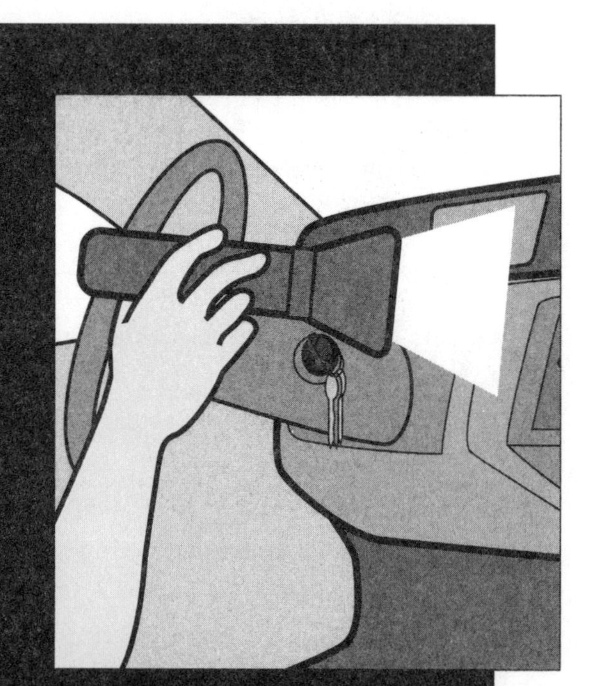

[7] Your final step in the vehicle bomb search is an exploration of the dashboard. Do this only after you have inspected the vehicle's exterior and interior, the trunk, and the engine. Use a flashlight to look into the air ducts. Look at the turn signals and lights; if nothing is unusual, turn them on. Check and test the wipers, washer, radio, and horn. If all of these seem to be in normal working order, you may start the car. Run the engine for two minutes before you begin your journey.

Commercial Buses, Trains, and Taxis

Most people who travel to foreign countries probably do not have access to their own vehicles. In this case, you will end up using public transportation of some kind. Be careful.

- Try to travel with a companion.
- Vary mode of commercial transportation.
- Select busy stops.
- Do not always use the same taxi company.
- Do not let someone you don't know direct you to a specific cab.
- Ensure that any taxi in which you ride is licensed and has safety equipment (seatbelts at the very least).
- Ensure that the face of the driver matches the photograph on his or her license or identification.
- If possible, specify the route you want the taxi to follow.

Safeguards while Walking

Of course, sometimes you will want to walk or will have to travel on foot.

- Be alert to the possibility of surveillance. Before leaving a building or mode of transportation, check up and down the street for suspicious-looking cars or individuals. (For more information, see *"Detecting Surveillance," below.*)

- Walk facing traffic at all times.
- Walk on the center of the sidewalk so you can see around corners. Walking next to the street affords someone the opportunity to push you out into the street.
- Remain alert when walking across alley entrances or other places where a terrorist or criminal could be hiding.
- Walk only in lighted areas. Avoid bad sections of town.
- Avoid walking in noisy areas, e.g., construction sites.
- Stay near people. Don't walk in isolated areas, e.g., alleys.
- Avoid hostile crowds by turning back or crossing the street.
- If you suspect you are being followed, move as quickly as possible to a safe haven (e.g., police station or government office).

DETECTING SURVEILLANCE

Terrorist operations are normally meticulously planned, allowing for the greatest chance of success and safe escape for the terrorists. Reducing vulnerability with security enhancements is vital to your efforts to deter terrorist attacks. Equally important is surveillance detection. In most cases, the target that terrorists select is based on lengthy surveillance. Through surveillance, they hope to learn about your habits and assess where you are vulnerable. By practicing good individual protective measures, you not only disrupt their intelligence-gathering efforts, but also make yourself a hard target. Terrorists want to hit soft targets, which minimizes their risk of failure. In cases of targets of opportunity, however, the surveillance may last for only a few minutes or hours to confirm the ease of the target. However, terrorists will usually abandon hard targets and move on to another soft target.

Upon arrival in a new area, begin determining what is normal and routine. Once you've determined this, it is easier to recognize what is unusual. This makes the problem of identifying surveillance simpler.

Often, initial surveillance efforts are conducted by less experienced personnel who may often make mistakes. For example, terrorists will often show up at a surveillance location immediately prior to their target's arrival and depart immediately after the target leaves. A counter-surveillance program involving family members, neighbors, and domestic employees can often detect this surveillance:

- Look for people who are in the wrong place or dressed inappropriately.
- Eliminate stereotypes about terrorist surveillance personnel; they are often women and children.
- Be particularly observant when traveling to and from your home or office.
- Look up and down the streets for suspicious vehicles, including motorcycles, mopeds, and bicycles.
- Note people near your home or place of work who appear to be repair personnel, utility crews, or even peddlers. Ask yourself if they appear genuine or whether they are unusual in any way.

Types of Surveillance

- Stationary: at home, along route, or at work
- Following: on foot or by vehicle
- Monitoring: telephone, mail, computers
- Searching: luggage, personal effects, trash
- Eavesdropping: electronic and personnel

Terrorists sometimes employ an elaborate system involving several people and vehicles. Typical surveillance vehicles are motorcycles and cars with multiple personnel. Become familiar with local vehicle makes and models. Memorize and write down license plate numbers. Determine if a surveillance pattern is developing.

Surveillance Indicators

- Illegally parked or occupied parked vehicles
- Cars with large mirrors
- Cars that suddenly pull out of parking places or side streets when you pass, cars that move with you when you move, or cars that pass you and immediately park
- Cars slowly maneuvering through turns and intersections or vehicles signaling for turns but not turning
- Flashing lights for signaling between cars
- Unusual speeding up, slowing down, or running red lights to keep up with you

Conduct analyses of the principal routes that you take on routine trips. Identify choke points where your vehicle must slow down. Typically, these include traffic circles, one-way streets, bridges, and major intersections. Search out safe havens along your routes that you can pull into in the event of emergency. If you think you're being followed, go directly to a safe haven, not to your home. Safe havens are generally well-lighted, public facilities where there are people who can respond to your request for help. (Examples include police stations, firehouses, large shopping malls, and busy restaurants.)

If you are aware of surveillance, never let those watching you know you have figured out what they are doing. Never confront them. Terrorists and criminal elements are typically armed, don't want to be identified, and may react violently in a confrontation.

Reaction (if in a Vehicle)

- Check during turns or circle the block for confirmation of surveillance.
- Do not stop or take other actions that could lead to confrontation
- If possible, get a description of the car and its occupants.
- Do not go home. Instead, go to the nearest safe haven. Report incident to the nearest law enforcement organization.

Reaction (if on Foot)

- Move rapidly toward a safe haven, avoiding any route you routinely use.
- If a safe haven is not immediately available, move into a crowded area.
- Immediately report suspicions to local law enforcement.

CHAPTER 4

REACTION: AFTER THE ATTACK

Attack Recognition

If terrorists succeed in their surveillance and plan an attack, the next chance to foil their efforts is to recognize their intentions and prepare to escape. Recognizing an attack scenario is difficult. Often, what may appear to be an attack is more likely to be innocent circumstances. However, alertness and willingness to act are the keys to surviving a genuine attack scenario.

ABNORMAL SITUATIONS

- Individuals who appear to be excessively nervous and seem out of place because of dress or mannerisms
- Individuals wearing unusually long or heavy clothing for the environment
- Individuals who appear to be acting as lookouts along your route of travel
- Vehicles that hit your car from the front or rear.
- Unusual detours, vehicle roadblocks, cones, or other barriers. Be prepared to escape by going around an obstacle or ramming it
- Vehicles traveling with items protruding from side doors or vans traveling with side doors open
- Disabled vehicles, hitchhikers, or distressed "accident

victims" seeking your assistance

- A flagman, workman, or fake police or government checkpoint stopping your car at a suspicious place
- Sudden unusual activity or the unexplained absence of local civilians
- Gunfire

Incident Recognition and Reaction

Disaster preparedness is no longer the sole concern of those who live in earthquake-prone California and in the part of the country known as Tornado Alley. For Americans, preparedness must now account for man-made disasters as well as natural ones. Knowing what to do during an emergency is an important part of being prepared and may make all the difference when seconds count.

BIOLOGICAL ATTACK

In the event of a biological attack, public health officials will provide information on what you should do as quickly as they can. However, it can take time for them to determine exactly what the illness is, how it should be treated, and who is in danger. What you can do is watch television, listen to the radio, or check the Internet for official news, including the following:

- Are you in the group or area authorities consider in danger?
- What are the signs and symptoms of the disease?
- Are medications or vaccines being distributed?
- Where?
- Who should get them?
- Where should you seek emergency medical care if you become sick?

Protect Yourself

If you become aware of an unusual and suspicious release of an unknown substance nearby, it doesn't hurt to protect yourself. Be prepared to improvise to protect your nose, mouth, and eyes, as well as cuts in your skin.

- Cover your mouth and nose with layers of fabric that can filter the air without interfering with breathing. Anything that fits snugly over your nose and mouth, including any dense-weave cotton material, can help filter contaminants in an emergency. There are also a variety of face masks readily available in hardware

stores. In a pinch, several layers of tissue or paper towels may help. (For more detail, see *Chapter 3: "Make a Plan, page 68"*)
- Wash with soap and water.
- Contact authorities.

Creating a Barrier

Many agents must be inhaled, absorbed through cuts in the skin, or eaten to make you sick. They can only hurt you if they get into your body, so think about creating a barrier between yourself and any contamination.

Symptoms and Hygiene

At the time of a declared biological emergency, if a family member becomes sick, it is important to be suspicious. Do not automatically assume, however, that you should go to a hospital emergency room or that any illness is the result of the biological attack. Symptoms of many common illnesses may overlap with those caused by biological attack. Use common sense, practice good hygiene and cleanliness to avoid spreading germs, and seek medical advice.

COMMON SENSE

There are a number of basic things that a person or

family can and should do when a family member becomes ill, whether the illness is the result of a terrorist attack or a normal source of infection.

- Maintain healthy habits.
- Eat well.
- Get plenty of rest.
- In a declared biological emergency or developing epidemic, there may be reason to stay away from crowds where others may be infected.
- There may be times when you would want to consider wearing a face mask to reduce spreading germs if you yourself are sick, or to avoid coming in contact with contagious germs if others around you are sick.

SYMPTOMS

If a family member develops any of the symptoms below, keep them separated from others if possible, practice good hygiene and cleanliness to avoid spreading germs, and seek medical advice.

- A temperature of more than 100 degrees
- Nausea and vomiting
- Stomachache

- Diarrhea
- Pale or flushed face
- Headache
- Cough
- Earache
- Thick discharge from nose
- Sore throat
- Rash or infection of the skin
- Red or pink eyes
- Loss of appetite
- Loss of energy or decreases in activity

HYGIENE

If someone is sick, you should practice good hygiene and cleanliness to avoid spreading germs.

- Wash your hands with soap and water frequently.
- Do not share food or utensils.
- Cover your mouth and nose when coughing or sneezing.
- Consider having the sick person wear a face mask to avoid spreading germs.
- Plan to share health-related information with others, especially those who may need help understanding the situation and what specific actions to take.

ANTIBIOTICS

While antibiotics are often an appropriate treatment for the diseases associated with biological weapons, the specific drug must match the illness to be effective. One antibiotic, for example, may be appropriate for treating anthrax exposure but inappropriate for treating smallpox. All antibiotics can cause side effects, which can be quite serious. Speak with your health care provider in advance about what makes sense for your family.

BIOLOGICAL ATTACK

In the case of a suspected biological attack, follow these simple steps.

[1] A biological attack is the deliberate release of germs or other biological substances that can make people ill or kill them. Biological agents can be delivered by inhalation, through a cut in the skin, or via ingestion (eating or drinking). Some biological agents can cause contagious diseases; others affect only the people with whom they make direct contact.

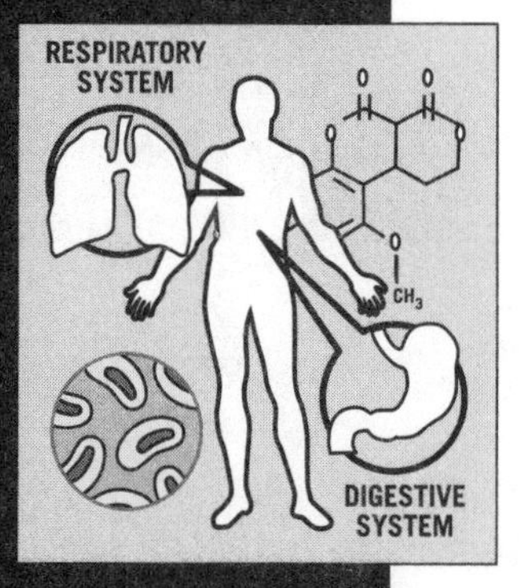

[2] A biological attack may or may not be immediately obvious. Although it is possible for a person to see signs of a biological attack, it is more likely that it will become apparent only when local health-care workers report a pattern of unusual illness. You will probably learn of the danger through an emergency radio or television broadcast. You may also become aware of it through Internet news or a phone call from a friend.

[3] If you become aware of the release of an unusual or suspicious substance nearby, there are three steps you should take right away. First, get away from the substance as quickly as possible.

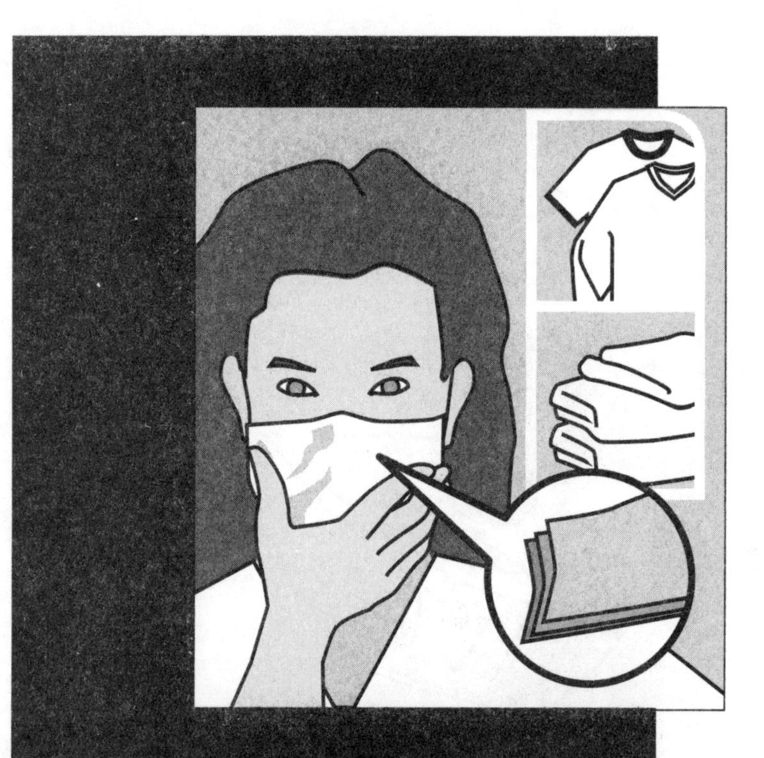

[4] Second, cover your mouth and nose with layers of fabric to filter the air. Make sure that this makeshift filter does not interfere with your breathing.

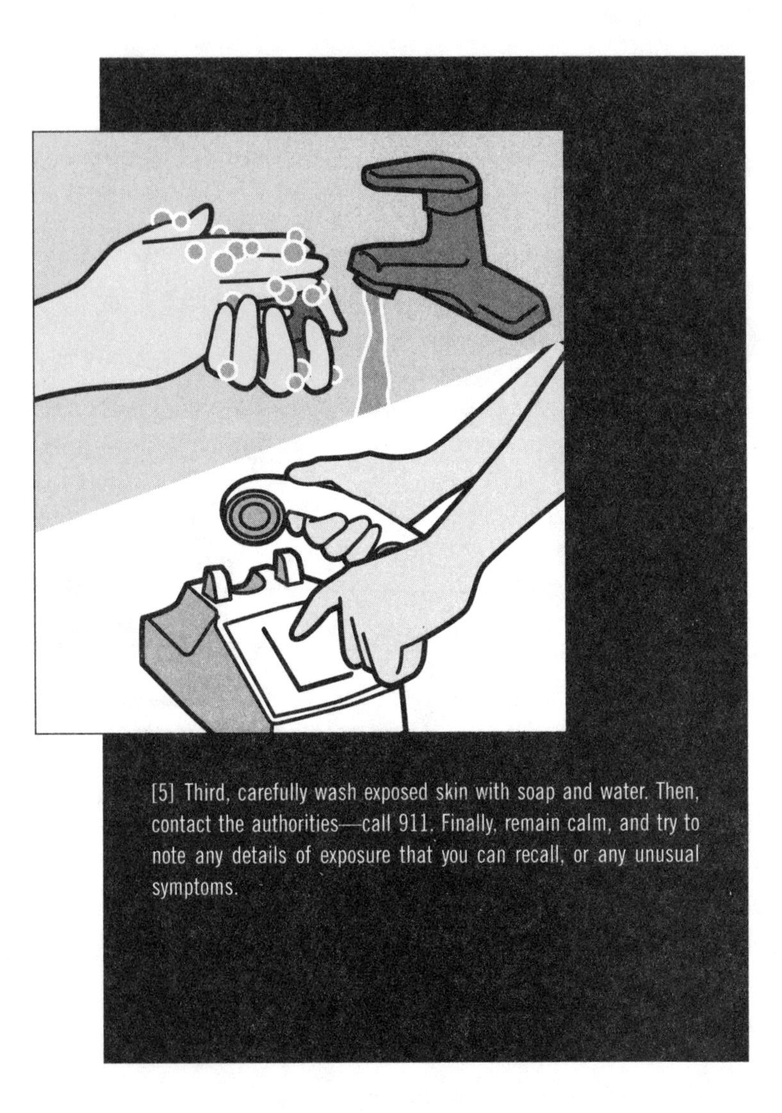

[5] Third, carefully wash exposed skin with soap and water. Then, contact the authorities—call 911. Finally, remain calm, and try to note any details of exposure that you can recall, or any unusual symptoms.

[6] In the event of a biological attack, public health officials may not immediately be able to provide information on your best course of action. You should watch television, listen to the radio, or check the Internet for official news.

[7] If a biological emergency is declared, be suspicious but do not automatically assume that any illness is a result of the attack. Symptoms of many common illnesses may overlap with those of diseases spread by a biological weapon. Use common sense, practice good hygiene and cleanliness to avoid spreading germs, and seek medical advice.

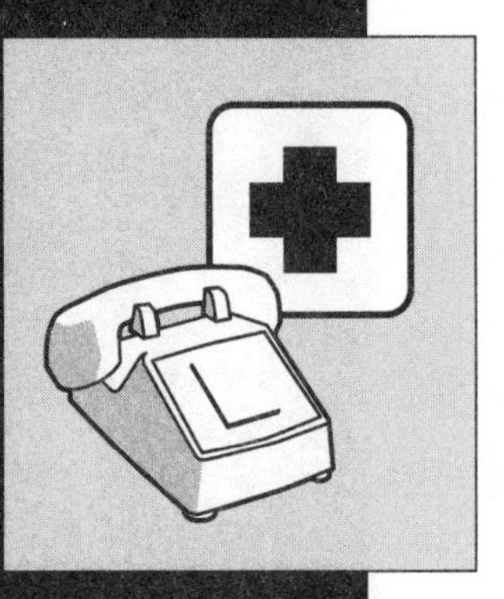

CHEMICAL ATTACK

A chemical attack is the deliberate release of a toxic gas, liquid, or solid that can poison people and the environment.

Protection of breathing airways is the single most important thing to address in the event of a chemical attack. In most cases, absent a gas mask, the only sure way to protect an airway is to put distance between you and the source of the agent. While evacuating the area, cover your mouth and nose with a handkerchief, coat sleeve, or any piece of cloth to provide some moderate means of protection.

CHEMICAL ATTACK

In the case of a suspected chemical attack, follow these simple steps.

[1] A chemical attack is the deliberate release of a toxic gas, liquid, or solid that can poison people, their environment, or both. Depending on how the chemical is delivered, a great many people can be affected at once.

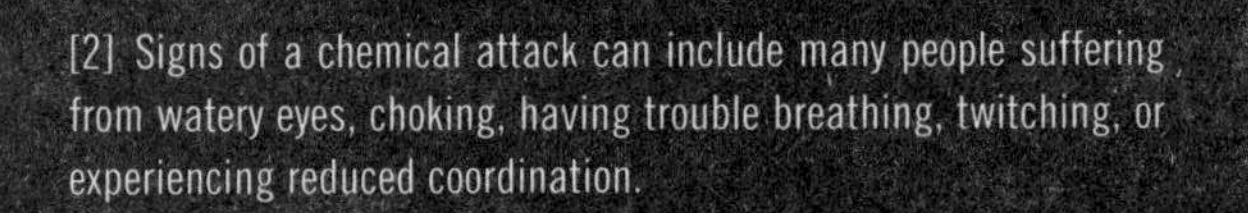

[2] Signs of a chemical attack can include many people suffering from watery eyes, choking, having trouble breathing, twitching, or experiencing reduced coordination.

[3] Large numbers of sick or dead birds, fish, or small animals are also cause for suspicion. Do not touch any of the affected creatures; instead note the circumstances of where you saw them, then inform the authorities.

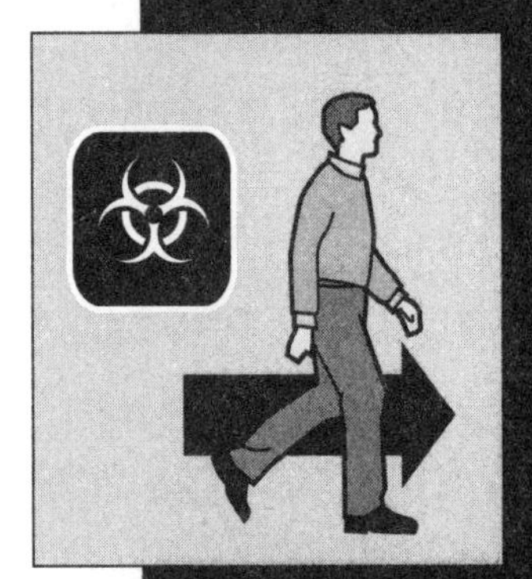

[4] If you see signs of a chemical attack, try to determine the size and shape of the affected area, and the chemical's origin. Do not spend too much time on this; if it is not immediately apparent, leave the area and contact the authorities.

[5] If the chemical is inside the building you are in, try to get out of the building without passing through the contaminated area. Move outdoors or to an interior room or a higher floor. Remember, many agents are heavier than air and will tend to stay close to the ground.

[6] If you cannot escape the area without risking contamination, move as far as possible from the suspected location of the chemical release and "shelter in place." If you can do so without endangering yourself, close all windows and exterior doors, and shut down the air-conditioning or heating system to prevent circulation of possibly contaminated air.

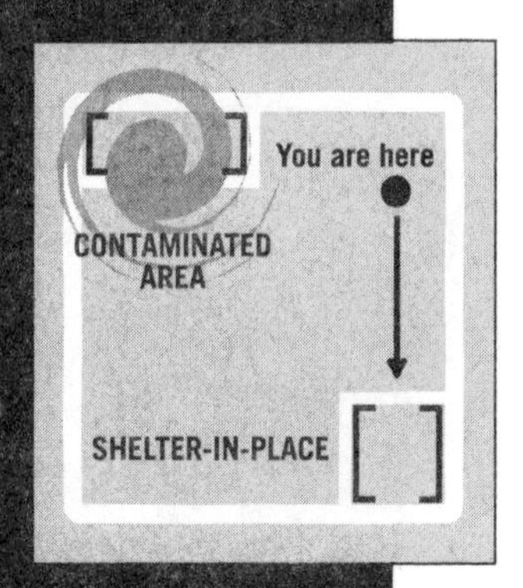

[7] If you are outside when you see signs of a chemical attack, try to determine the fastest way to distance yourself from the chemical threat. In any case, try to move upwind of the source.

[8] Depending on where you are in relation to the affected area, it might be better to go inside a building and "shelter in place."

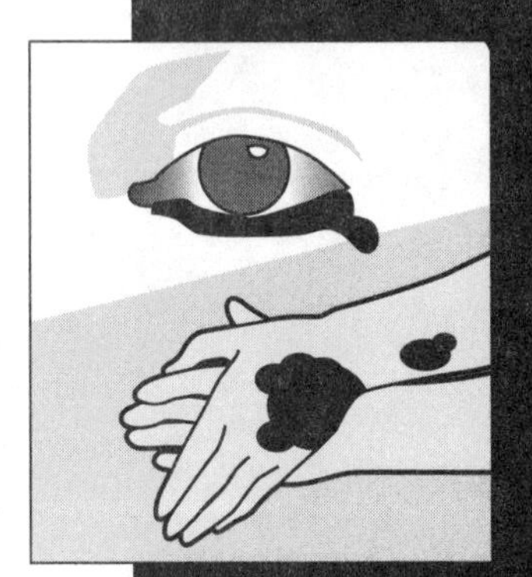

[9] If your eyes are watering, your skin is stinging, you are having trouble breathing, or for any reason you think you might have been exposed to a chemical, you should immediately strip down and clean your entire body.

[10] Look for a hose, a fountain, a sink, or any source of water. Wash with soap and water, if possible, but do not scrub—that might push the chemical into your skin instead of cleaning it off. Even better, use a diluted bleach solution (10 parts water to one part bleach). If water is not available, talcum powder or flour are also excellent means of decontamination of liquid agents. Sprinkle the flour or powder liberally over the affected skin area, wait 30 seconds, and gently wipe it off with a rag or gauze pad.

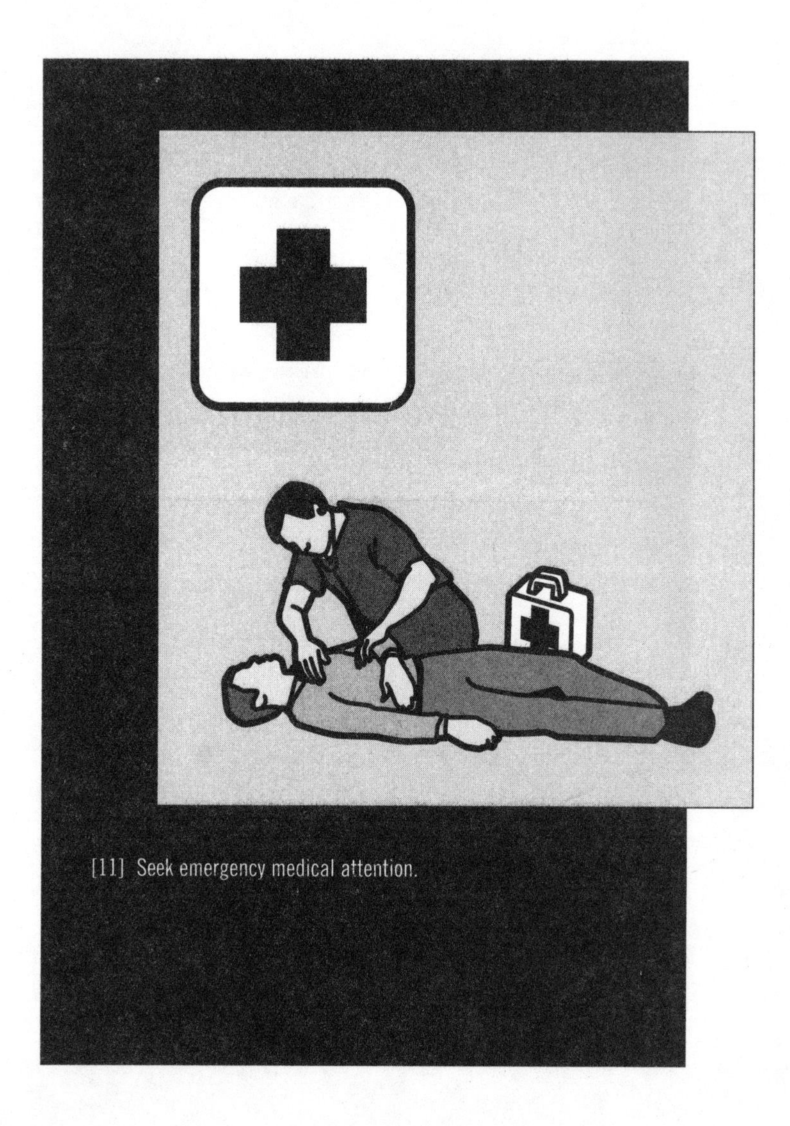

[11] Seek emergency medical attention.

NUCLEAR BLAST

You will know there has been a nuclear blast when you see a flash or a fireball. In order to limit the amount of radiation you are exposed to, think about shielding, distance, and time.

The first and most important thing to do is to take cover, below ground if you can. After that, you can use available information to assess the situation. If there is a significant radiation threat, health care authorities may or may not advise you to take potassium iodide. Potassium iodide is the same stuff added to your table salt to make it iodized. It may or may not protect your thyroid gland, which is particularly vulnerable to radioactive iodine exposure. Consider keeping potassium iodide in your emergency kit, and learn what the appropriate doses are for each of your family members. Plan to speak with your health care provider in advance about what makes sense for your family.

NUCLEAR BLAST

In the case of a suspected nuclear blast, follow these simple steps.

[1] If you find yourself in the area of a nuclear blast, take cover immediately. It is best to be below ground, but any shield or shelter will help protect you from the immediate effects of the blast and the pressure wave.

[2] **SHIELDING:** A thick shield between you and the radioactive materials will absorb some of the radiation, thus reducing your exposure.

[3] Try to determine the fastest way to distance yourself from the area. Remain calm, and try to coordinate with other people who are also leaving the area.

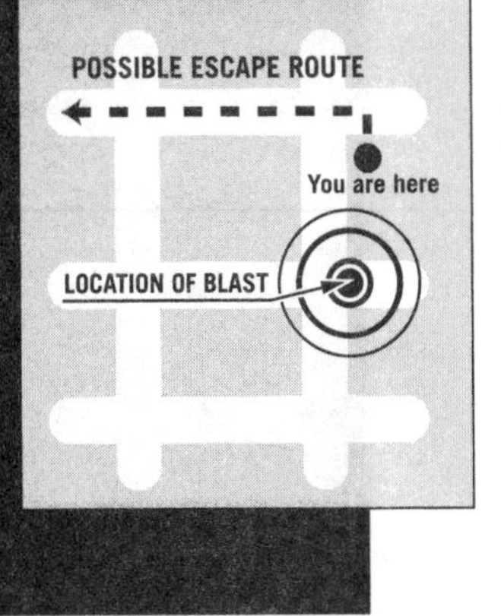

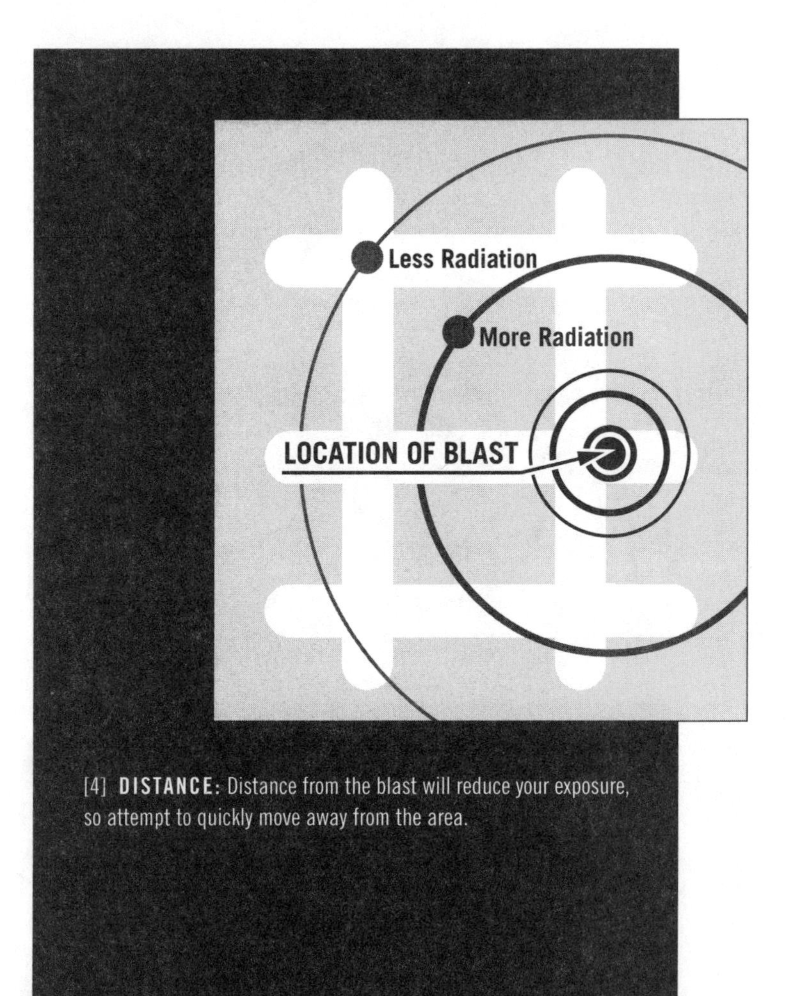

[4] **DISTANCE:** Distance from the blast will reduce your exposure, so attempt to quickly move away from the area.

[5] **TIME:** Minimization of time spent exposed will also reduce the risks associated with exposure to radiation.

[6] Depending on where you are in relation to the affected area, it might be better to go inside a building and "shelter in place."

RADIATION ATTACK ("DIRTY BOMB")

Remember, a radiation attack, or "dirty bomb," is not the same as a nuclear blast. It is instead the spreading of radioactive materials over a targeted area via the use of common explosives. Radioactive contamination from a dirty bomb will be much less widespread than that from a nuclear blast, but while the blast will be immediately apparent, the presence of radiation will not be clearly defined until trained personnel with specialized equipment are on the scene. As with any radiation, you want to try to limit exposure. Think about shielding, distance, and time.

RADIATION ATTACK

In the case of a suspected dirty bomb attack, follow these simple steps.

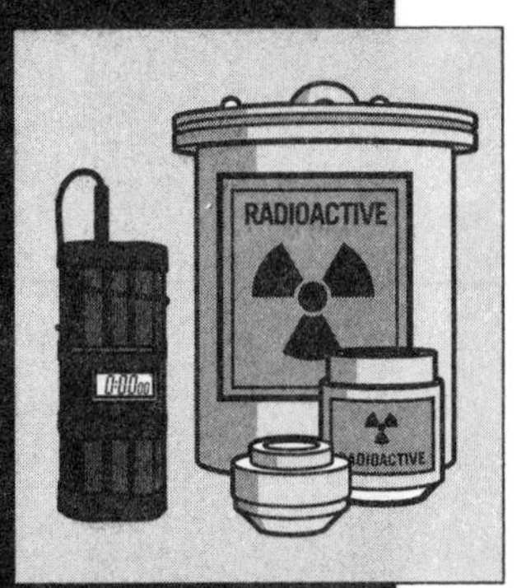

[1] A radiation attack, or "dirty bomb," is the use of common explosives to spread radioactive materials.

[2] Unlike in a nuclear blast, the force of the explosion and contamination from a radioactive attack will be localized. In order to limit your exposure to radiation, think about shielding, distance, and time.

[3] **SHIELDING:** A thick shield between you and the radioactive materials will absorb some of the radiation, thus reducing your exposure.

[4] **DISTANCE:** Distance from the blast will reduce your exposure, so attempt to move quickly away from the area.

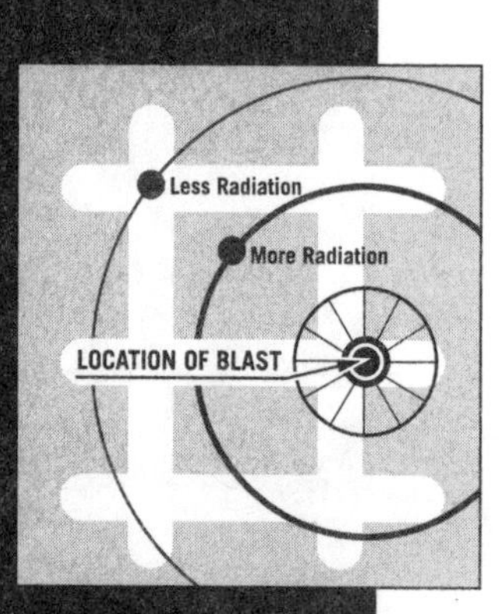

[5] **TIME:** Minimization of time spent exposed will also reduce the risks associated with exposure to radiation.

[6] In the event of a radiation attack, local authorities may not be able to immediately provide information on your best course of action. You should watch television, listen to the radio, or check the Internet for official news.

BOMBINGS

Should a bomb explode outside your building, do not rush to the window to see what happened. Immediately seek cover in a protected area; it is possible that a secondary, probably larger explosion may occur very soon after the first. Terrorists may use an initial bomb to breach outer security, then a second bomb on the target, and may follow up the bombing with an armed attack. In a variation, terrorists can set off an initial bomb, followed by a second bomb shortly thereafter to kill or injure security forces and emergency services responding to the initial bomb.

In the city, if you are on the street when a terrorist bomb explosion occurs, quickly get inside the nearest building and remain there. Shattered glass and other debris from high-rise buildings can fall for blocks around the point of explosion. Following a bombing of any kind, do the following as soon as it is practical to do so:

- Notify the proper authorities.
- Evacuate the wounded based on the situation. Do not impede the efforts of emergency services. Witnesses to the bombing will naturally approach the explosion area to aid in searching for casualties. Authorities will also be trying to coordinate the search and will want

to limit the number of searchers due to the threat of additional explosions and secondary effects such as falling masonry or fires.

- Move to a clear area, away from objects such as automobiles, buildings, and garbage containers.

EXPLOSIONS

If there is an explosion...

[1] Take shelter under your desk, if it's of strong wood or metal construction, or under a sturdy table. Otherwise, seek shelter in a doorway.

[2] Exit the building as quickly as possible. If time allows, take your emergency survival kit with you.

[3] Do not use elevators. When there is an explosion, a fire, or any structural damage to tall buildings, elevators can be shut down or disabled, and their cables and safety features can be weakened. Use the stairs to make your way to the exit, but be careful—stairs may be weakened, electrical wires may be exposed, and other hazards may have been created by the incident.

EXPLOSIONS

If there is a fire...

[1] Exit the building as quickly as possible. If time allows, take your emergency survival kit with you.

[2] If the room or hallway fills with smoke, crawl along the ground to avoid breathing it in. Most injuries incurred in a fire are the result of smoke inhalation.

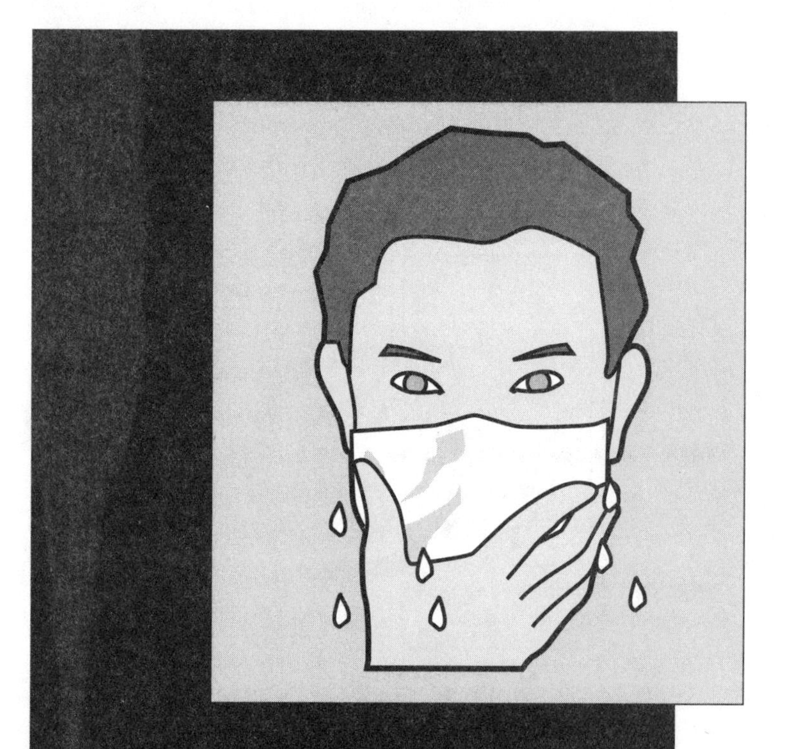

[3] Use a wet cloth to cover your nose and mouth; this will help to filter the smoke.

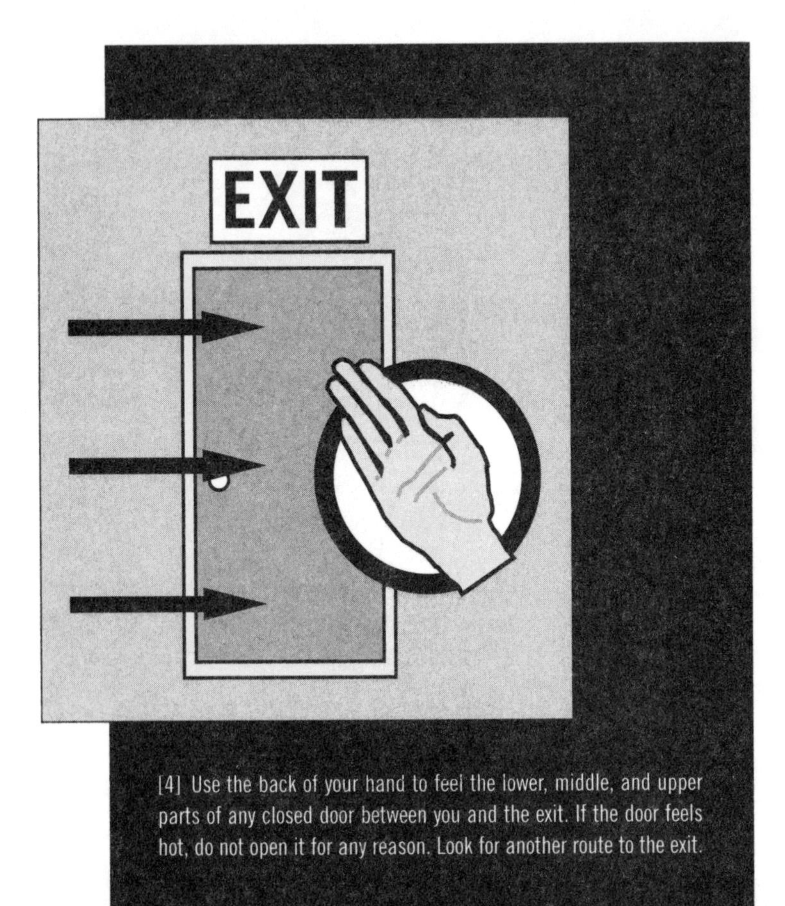

[4] Use the back of your hand to feel the lower, middle, and upper parts of any closed door between you and the exit. If the door feels hot, do not open it for any reason. Look for another route to the exit.

[5] If a door is not hot, you may proceed. Brace yourself against the door and open it slowly.

[6] If a door is hot, leave it closed. A hot door indicates fire burning in the room behind it; if you open the door, the fire will spread into the room where you are. Look for another way out.

[7] Do not use elevators. When there is an explosion, a fire, or any structural damage to tall buildings, elevators can be shut down or disabled, and their cables and safety features can be weakened. Use the stairs to make your way to the exit, but be careful—stairs may be weakened, electrical wires may be exposed, and other hazards may have been created by the incident.

[8] If you or your clothing catches fire, do not run. Running only fans the flames, intensifying the fire and causing greater damage.

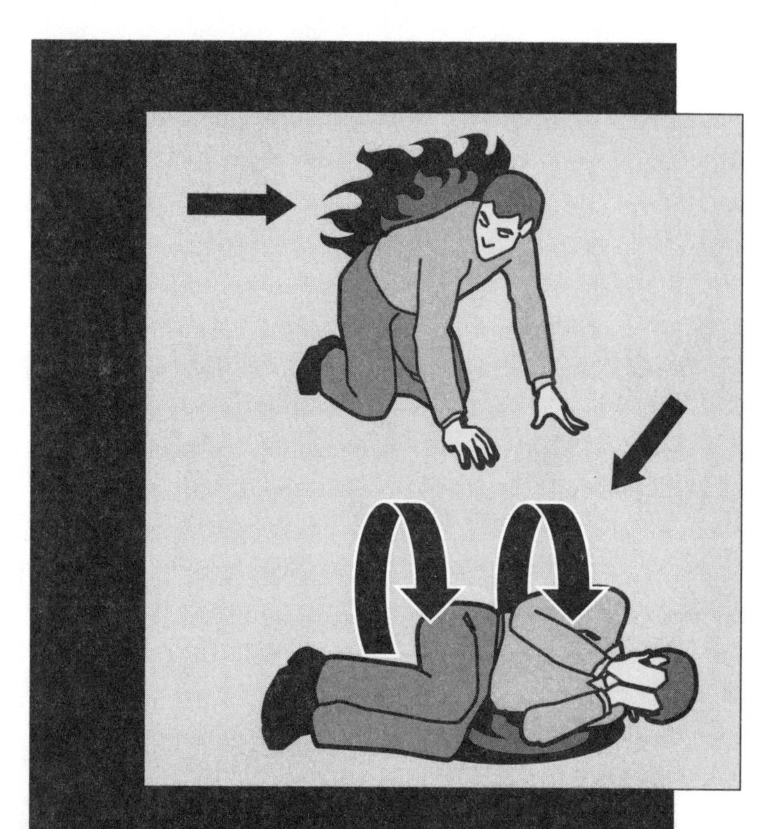

[9] Stop, drop, and roll. It's the most effective response to a fire on you or your clothes. When your body presses against the ground, it makes it harder for the fire to spread. If you have a heavy coat or blanket, try to smother the flames.

[10] If you are at home when an explosion occurs, go to your previously designated meeting place.

[11] Account for all of your family members; make sure that children are carefully supervised at such moments. Find your pets; follow your emergency plan for them.

[12] Never go back into a burning building. Even if you have left valuables or pets behind, do not enter the building. Wait for firefighters to arrive on the scene; they will do their best to save your house and will, if it is within their power, work to save any creatures still trapped inside.

[13] Call the fire department.

EXPLOSIONS

If you are trapped in debris...

[1] Use a flashlight, if possible, to signal your location.

[2] Avoid unnecessary movement so that you don't kick up dust. Cover your mouth and nose with anything you have on hand. Densely woven cotton can create a good filter. Try to breathe only through the material.

[3] Tap on a pipe or wall so that rescuers can hear where you are.

[4] Use a whistle if one is available. Shout only as a last resort—shouting can cause a person to inhale dangerous amounts of dust. If you have a cellular phone with you and are able to get a signal, call 911 and tell them where you are and how you became trapped. If possible, explain the nature of the debris.

HIJACKINGS, SKYJACKINGS, AND KIDNAPPINGS

For responses to hijackings and skyjackings, see *Chapter 3: "Abroad," page 81*. For what to do if you are kidnapped, see *Chapter 5: The Hostage Situation.*

If you come under the control of terrorists, you must rapidly determine the terrorists' intent: to establish a bargaining position and elicit publicity or to carry out a suicide mission. The passengers on board the planes used in the September 11, 2001, attacks in the United States were not hostages in the traditional sense because the terrorists never intended to use them to achieve a bargaining position. Those passengers were simply on board a skyjacked aircraft that was being used for a suicide mission. In such situations, the techniques described in *"Escape or Surrender," page 192*, may be the most useful.

ARSON AND FIREBOMBS

Exercise normal fire-safety precautions. However, do not gather in open areas such as parking lots or areas where others are congregating. Terrorists could stage an arson attack or false fire alarm to get a crowd out of a building and then conduct a bombing or armed attack.

ARMED ATTACKS AND ASSASSINATIONS

If you are in an office or hotel when an armed attack or assassination takes place, quickly lock the door, turn out the lights, grab the telephone, and get down on the floor. Call building security immediately. Telephone connections outside the building or hotel might be difficult to obtain. If no security office is available, call the local authorities. Tell the authorities exactly what you heard and provide them with the address, building, floor, room number, and telephone number. Stay in a protected area, and if possible, take the phone with you.

Escape, Evade, or Confront

Once you realize that an attack is occurring, decisions must be made immediately. If the scenario is an armed attack or assassination attempt, get out of the kill zone. Typically, terrorists have a relatively narrow window of time and may have restricted fields of fire due to obstacles in their path. Once they have made their attempt, terrorists must begin their escape and evasion plan. If you are the target of such an attempt—which is very unlikely unless you are a highly placed government operative or elected official—it may be a matter of survival to employ evasive driving techniques in order to arrive at the nearest safe haven. Use of evasive driving techniques may also be to your advantage in that they will attract the attention of local law enforcement. If on foot, take advantage of the density of crowds and layouts of buildings to evade pursuers. When you feel you have evaded the terrorists and are out of immediate danger, contact local law enforcement for assistance.

In some cases, you may become captive, like the passengers on board the ill-fated flights of September 11, 2001. On those airplanes, escape and evasion were not possible. The only chance for those passengers to survive was to confront the terrorists and regain control. On one aircraft, although the plane crashed, killing all on board, the passengers' confrontation with the terrorists saved countless lives because the aircraft never reached its intended target.

DECIDING TO STAY OR GO

If a crisis arises, use available information to assess the situation. Remember, local authorities may not immediately be able to provide information on what is happening and what you should do. Use personal observation and watch television, listen to the radio, or check the Internet for breaking news and instructions. Depending on your circumstances and the nature of the attack, the first important decision is deciding whether to stay or go. Earlier in this book, you learned how to prepare for various eventualities. This section tells you what to do should those situations come to pass.

Staying Put

Use available information to assess the situation. If you see large amounts of debris in the air, or if local authorities say the air is badly contaminated, you may want to "shelter-in-place." You have already prepared for this situation; now, all you need to do is put those plans into motion:

- Bring your family and pets inside.
- Lock doors and close windows, air vents, and fireplace dampers.
- Turn off fans, air-conditioning, and forced-air heating systems.
- Take your emergency supply kit, unless you have reason to believe it has been contaminated.
- Go into an interior room with few windows, if possible.

- Seal all windows, doors, and air vents with prepared plastic sheeting and duct tape.
- Be prepared to improvise and use what you have on hand to seal gaps and create a barrier between yourself and any contamination.

Getting Away

There may be conditions under which you will decide to get away, or there may be moments when you are ordered to leave. You have already planned what to do in these cases; here is what to do if such a situation arises:

- Take your emergency supply kit, unless you believe it has been contaminated. Lock the door behind you.
- Take your pets with you, but understand that only service animals may be permitted in public shelters. (see *Chapter 3: "Plan for Your Pets," page 75*).
- If you believe the outside air may be contaminated, drive with your windows and vents closed and keep the air-conditioning and heater turned off.
- Listen to the radio for instructions.

IF TIME ALLOWS

- Call or e-mail the "roll-call taker" in your family

communications plan. Tell them where you are going. (If you do not have time to do this before you leave, call them from the car, on your cellular phone.)

- If there is damage to your home and you are instructed to do so, shut off water, gas, and electricity before leaving.
- Leave a note telling others when you left and where you are going.
- Check with neighbors who may need a ride.

IN A MOVING VEHICLE

If you are in a moving vehicle when a terrorist attack occurs, follow these simple steps.

[1] If an incident occurs while you are in your automobile, use available information to evaluate the situation. If there is an explosion or other factor that makes it difficult to control the vehicle, pull over.

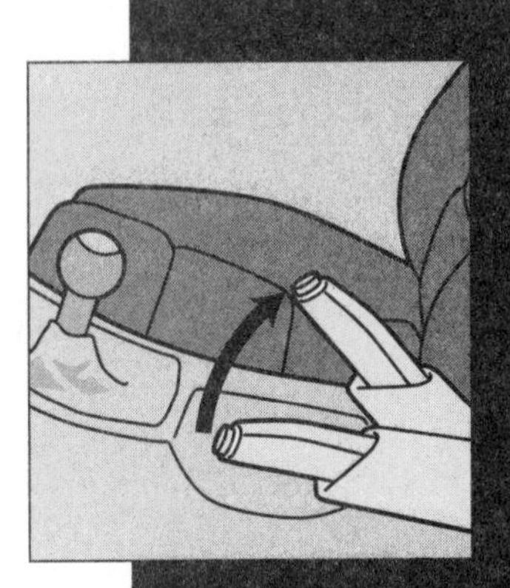

[2] Stop the car and set the parking brake. If you have been unable to stop, the emergency brake will help. Once stopped, the brake will keep your car in place until the emergency has passed or emergency personnel have arrived and cleared you for departure.

[3] If the emergency could undermine the physical stability of the roadway, avoid overpasses, bridges, power lines, signs, and other potential hazards. Your best bet, if you cannot be sure that your journey will not take you near or onto such danger zones, is to pull over until you know that the situation has been brought to a safe end.

[4] If a power line falls on your car, you are at risk of electrical shock. Stay inside the vehicle until a trained emergency worker removes the wire.

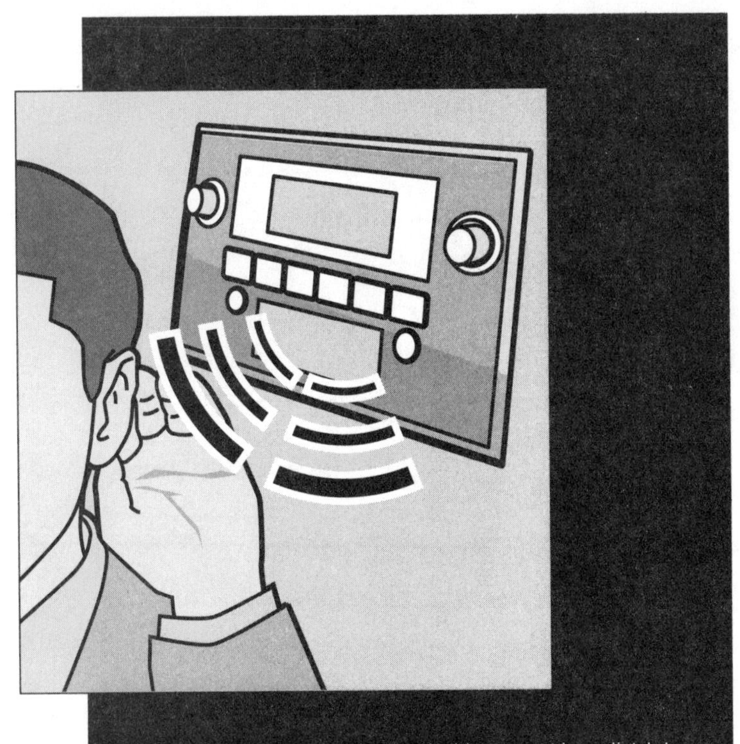

[5] As with any emergency, local authorities may not immediately be able to provide information on your best course of action. Listen to the radio for information.

IN A HIGH-RISE BUILDING

If you are in a high-rise building when a terrorist attack occurs, follow these simple steps.

[1] Use available information to evaluate the situation. Note the location of the closest emergency exit.

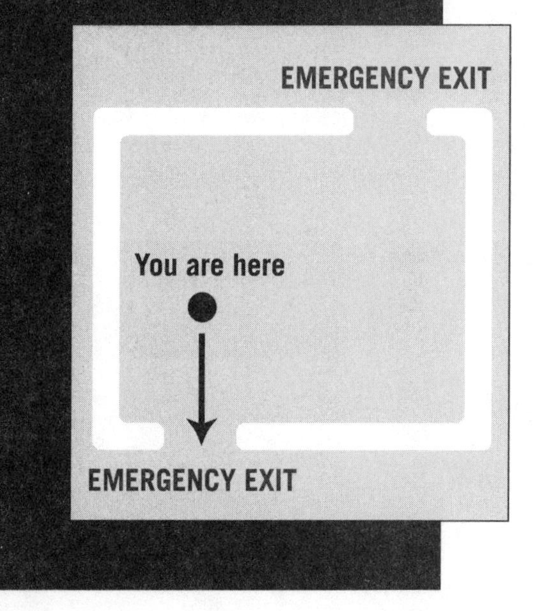

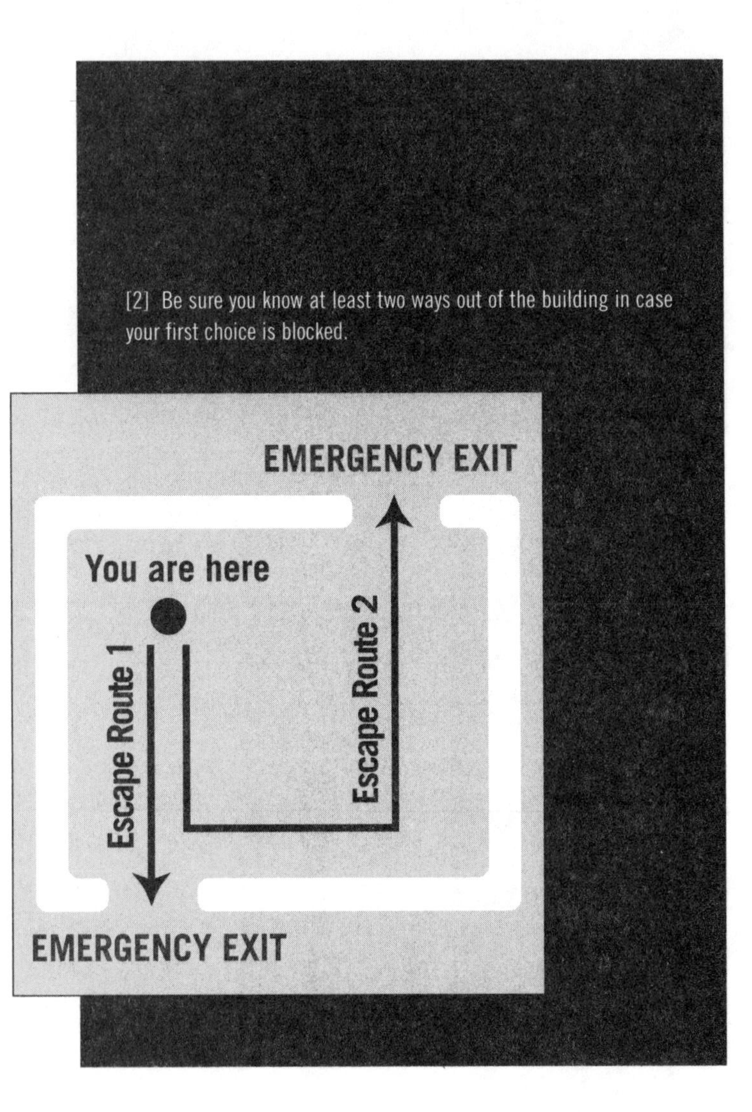
[2] Be sure you know at least two ways out of the building in case your first choice is blocked.
EMERGENCY EXIT
You are here
Escape Route 1
Escape Route 2
EMERGENCY EXIT

[3] If things are falling, take cover under a sturdy desk or table, preferably of strong wooden or metal construction. If this is not possible and you cannot escape to a safe place, stand close to the wall or in a doorway—this may afford you some protection from falling debris.

[4] Move away from file cabinets, bookshelves, or other office furniture that may fall and cause injury. Do not try to "rescue" documents or equipment; focus on protecting yourself and other people.

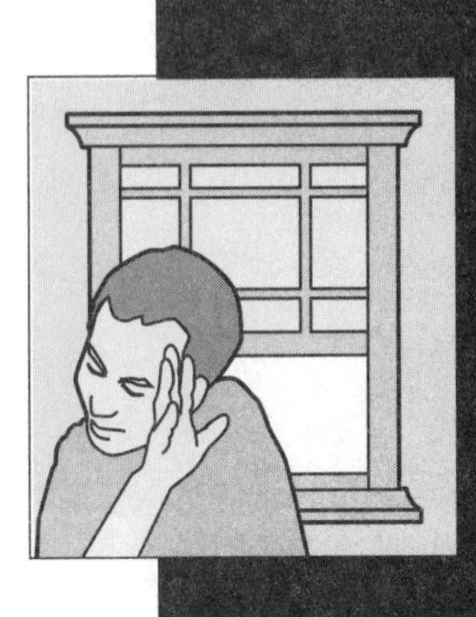

[5] Face away from windows and glass. Move away from exterior walls. If there are further explosions to come, windows can be blown inward and cause great injury.

[6] Determine whether you should stay put, "shelter in place," or get away. Listen for and follow instructions from authorities—call 911.

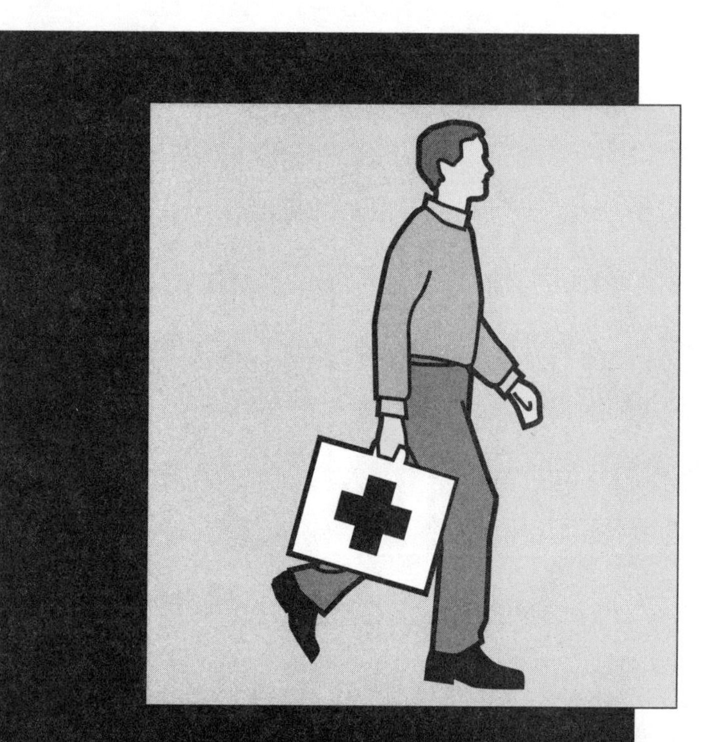

[7] Take your emergency supply kit unless there is reason to believe it has been contaminated.

[8] Do not use elevators. When there is an explosion, a fire, or any structural damage to tall buildings, elevators can be shut down or disabled, and their cables and safety features can be weakened. Use the stairs to make your way to the exit, but be careful—stairs may be weakened, electrical wires may be exposed, and other hazards may have been created by the incident.

[9] Stay to the right while going down stairways to allow emergency workers to come up the stairs into the building.

ESCAPE OR SURRENDER

If a terrorist attack occurs and you face capture, you will be faced with an important decision: escape or surrender. You will have very little time to make this decision. Even though the moment of capture is one of the most dangerous times of a hostage ordeal, you must remain calm. Do not make any sudden movement that may rattle an already anxious gunman. Abductors are tense; adrenaline is flowing. Terrorists themselves feel vulnerable until they are convinced that they have established firm control over their hostages. Unintentional violence can be committed with the slightest provocation. For example, do not make eye contact with the captors initially. Be polite and cooperate. You may need to reassure your abductors that you are not trying to escape by controlling your emotions, following instructions, and avoiding physical resistance.

Terrorists meticulously plan to capture hostages. Initiative, time, location, and circumstances of the capture usually favor the captors, not hostages. However, the best opportunity to escape is normally during the confusion of the takeover, while you are still in a relatively public place. During this period, the hostage-takers are focused on establishing control and may leave openings for escape.

Remember, mental alertness improves the chances of escape. While waiting for an opportunity to escape, continue passive information collection on the following:

- Appearance, accents, rank structure, equipment, and routines of the terrorists
- Strengths and weaknesses of the facility and its personnel
- Conditions and surrounding area that could have an impact on an escape attempt
- Items within the detention area that can be used to support an escape effort

Escape from detention by terrorists is risky but may become necessary if conditions deteriorate to the point that the risks associated with escape are less than the risks of remaining captive. These risks would include the credible threat of torture and death at the hands of the terrorists. Escape attempts should be made only after careful consideration of the risk of violence, chance of success, and possible detrimental effects on hostages remaining behind.

If you eliminate escape as an option, avoid physical resistance. Assure your captors of your intention to cooperate fully.

CHAPTER 5

THE HOSTAGE SITUATION

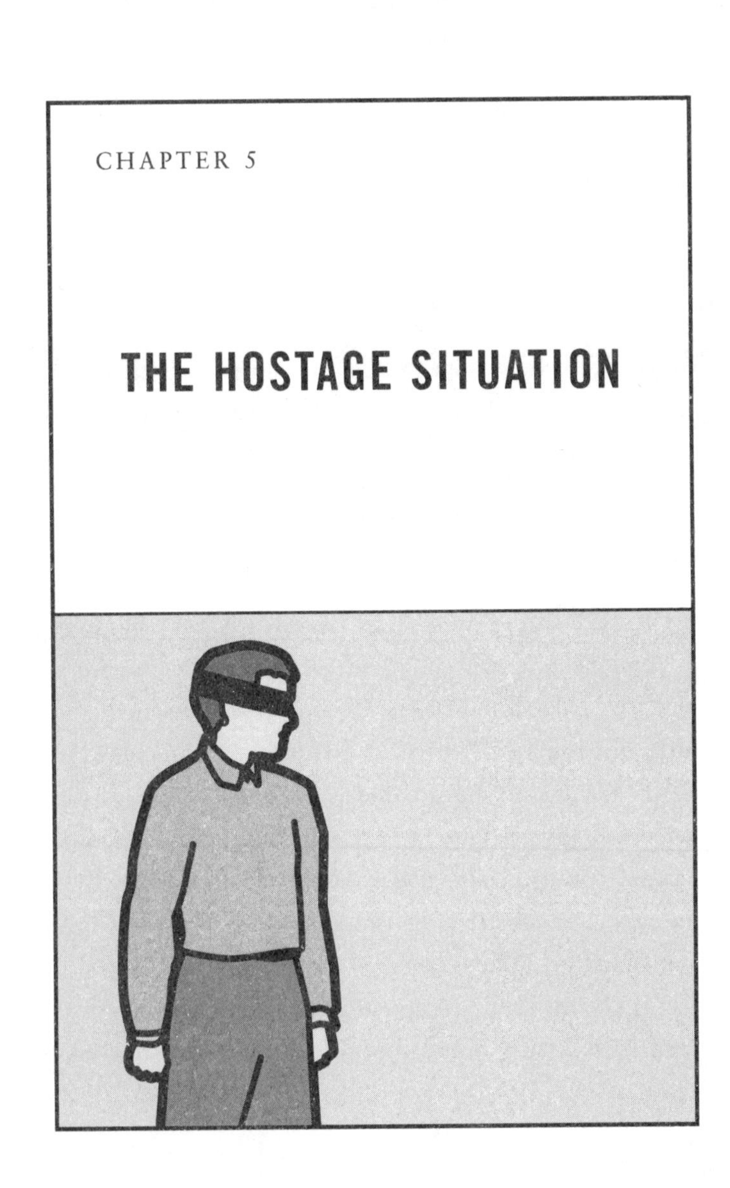

The Hostage

Hostage-taking is a way for terrorists to achieve a bargaining position by forcing a confrontation with authorities. It will remain an effective terrorist tool as long as mankind values human life. Hopefully, you will never become a hostage, but if you do, knowing how to react will improve your chances of survival.

Terrorists select hostages for a variety of reasons. The hostage may have a prominent job or social status or may be

- Well-known, so that the terrorists will receive widespread media attention by taking him or her hostage.
- An American.
- Hated by the terrorists. Alternately, the terrorists may blame the hostage for any setbacks inflicted on them by their own government's forces. For example, U.S. military advisors in El Salvador were despised by terrorists of the FMLN because the advisors provided assistance to the El Salvadoran government.
- Valuable to employers and families; for example, families and civilian firms have paid ransoms to secure a hostage's release.
- Seen as a threat to the terrorists. For example, in

Columbia, the terrorist groups M-19 and Revolutionary Armed Forces of Colombia (FARC), who make more than $100 million each year from cocaine sales, target special agents of the U.S. Drug Enforcement Administration.

These reasons identify why a particular person may be targeted for a hostage-taking. But in most cases, a hostage is an innocent victim of circumstances—someone who was in the wrong place at the wrong time. Remember, the chances of you being taken hostage are truly remote. Even better news is that survival rates are high. But should it happen, you must also remember that your personal conduct can influence treatment in captivity. Therefore, you must prepare yourself to respond (both mentally and physically) to a hostage-taking incident.

The Hostage-Takers

The following paragraphs address broad categories of hostage-takers—the ones that are the norm. The lines between the categories may blur or overlap, and the hostage-taker may move from one category to another based on a goal. Multiple subsets may also exist within each category.

POLITICAL EXTREMIST

Most hostage-takers are political extremists. They typically operate within a military-type structure. Their operations are usually well-planned. They typically resist appeals based on morals, decency, or fear for their own safety. They are often prepared to die for their cause.

Statistically, leaders of political extremist groups are single, urban, bright, and dedicated to their cause. They are often college graduates with professional backgrounds. They often come from upper or upper-middle class families and have parents who are politically active but not violent. They tend to be abnormally idealistic and inflexible.

FLEEING CRIMINAL

Fleeing criminals take hostages on impulse, typically to avoid immediate apprehension and to have a bargaining chip for escape. Authorities must handle a fleeing criminal with caution. If he or she feels a sudden loss of power, agitation, despair, or panic may ensue. With these emotions at the forefront, the criminal may impulsively kill a hostage. Therefore, time and patience in dealing with the hostage-taker is critical. The fleeing criminal will often settle for much less than originally demanded if he perceives that he is slowly losing power or control of the situation, or is facing death. Many times, he will surrender if allowed to give up with dignity.

WRONGED PERSON

A hostage-taker who feels he is a wronged person is motivated by personal revenge. He seeks to notify society of the defects in the system or the establishment. His actions are motivated by a desire to right a wrong or to publicize what he feels is an injustice. The hostage may represent the "system" to the hostage-taker; if so, the hostage could be in increased danger. This type of hostage-taker is convinced that he is absolutely right in his behavior. Often, gentle persuasion is required to convince him that he needs to end the situation and release the hostage.

RELIGIOUS EXTREMIST

Dealing with hostage-takers who are religious extremists requires time, patience, and sensitivity. Religious extremists share a common, unshakable belief in the righteousness of their cause. They may perceive that their source of power comes from their god or the leaders of their cult or group. They may see themselves as superior to others simply because of their beliefs. Individuals who join cults or radical religious groups often lack personal confidence and join these types of organizations to bolster their self-esteem.

Religious extremists may feel that they must succeed or die for their faith. Some religious cults and groups believe that to die at the hand of the nonbeliever is the holiest achievement possible. This way of thinking greatly increases the threat to the hostage. The hostage may also be seen as a "sacrificial lamb," one who must die for the sins of others.

MENTALLY DISTURBED INDIVIDUAL

A hostage-taker who is mentally disturbed is not normally associated with an organized terrorist group. However, this type of hostage-taker is responsible for over half of the hostage-taking incidents. Usually, the mentally disturbed hostage-taker acts alone. Authorities may have difficulty establishing and maintaining a rapport with the mentally disturbed hostage-taker. If challenged or threatened by authorities, the mentally disturbed hostage-taker may easily accept the murder of a hostage, his own suicide, or both.

Intimidation and Control

Remember, hostage-takers usually want you alive. They may use drugs, blindfolds, or gags when they abduct you, but try not to be alarmed or to resist unduly. If you struggle, hostage-takers may resort to more severe measures of restraint. Hostage-takers use blindfolds or hoods to keep you from knowing where you are being taken, as well as to prevent you from identifying them later. You should not attempt to remove a blindfold or hood; if you see your abductors, they may kill you. Likewise, you should not attempt to remove an abductor's mask or hood if they are wearing one.

Hostage-takers may also drug their victims, usually at the beginning of an operation, to make the victim sleep and keep him pacified. This experience should not be alarming. At this stage, your life is almost as important to the hostage-taker as it is to you. Drugs used to put you to sleep do not have lasting side effects. If hostage-takers should use drugs such as heroin, lysergic acid diethylamide (LSD), or sleeping pills, you can typically recover from this more quickly than you can from physical abuse.

Stabilization

If you are abducted, your goal is to survive. To survive,

you must adjust. You must try to regain emotional control as quickly as possible after the capture. Maintaining emotional control helps you keep control of your mental abilities, such as situational awareness, judgment, and decision-making skills. Remember, most hostages survive an abduction. After the initial shock of capture wears off, both hostage-takers and victims stabilize their emotions and begin to plan for the future. The terrorists may divulge information about themselves, their organization, their goals, and their objectives. They may share their demands and may even discuss roles and responsibilities that the hostages have. The hostages begin making an emotional transition from being a victim to being a survivor. But to survive, you must be alert and cautious. Remember that hostage-takers have been known to use "sleepers" in their hostage operations. A sleeper is a terrorist posing as a hostage to inform on the real hostages or to draw out security personnel. Be careful whom you trust.

SITUATIONAL AWARENESS

If you are blindfolded and gagged during transportation, concentrate on sounds, smells, direction of movement, passage of time, conversations of the hostage-takers, and any other information that might be useful. For example, you might hear train sounds, indicating that you are near a train station or going by railroad tracks. Hearing a ship's horn would tell you that you are crossing a river or that you are near a body of water. Try and draw a mental map of where you are. If you can hear the hostage-takers, try to determine what language they are speaking, key phrases, goals of the abduction, names, weapons carried, and directions taken, such as "make a left at [famous landmark]." Information collected over time might allow you to guess the possible route and the area where they have taken you. All this information will be very useful if you are released or if you escape while the hostage-takers are still holding other hostages.

CONFRONTATIONS

Do your best to avoid confrontations with any hostage-taker. If taken hostage, you must be prepared to explain telephone numbers, addresses, names, and any other items carried at the time of capture. If interrogated, adopt a simple, tenable position and stick with it. You should try to convince your captors that they have kidnapped the wrong person. The terrorists may not be convinced, but don't give up. This delaying effort serves only to maximize survival during the initial stages of captivity and reduce the terrorist's apprehension that you might be a threat to their activities. Most casualties among hostages occur during the process of capture and initial internment.

Defense Mechanisms

It is important to understand what is going on in the minds of hostages, including yourself. You might observe what you would consider unusual behavior. This behavior is usually a combination of psychological effects that terrorists seek to achieve by their controlling actions and unconscious, personality-based responses hostages display while in captivity.

Survival is instinctively the most important issue to the human mind. When placed in a hostage situation, the mind commonly employs defense mechanisms. These unconscious psychological adjustments are made by hostages to deal with the stress and trauma of the situation. To survive this ordeal, the mind can typically deny that the incident is occurring; regress into a dependent state; and/or identify with the hostage-taker's demands and values to avoid punishment. A combination of these defense mechanisms can result in the "Stockholm Syndrome," whereby the hostage identifies with the hostage-taker and may actively support his or her activities.

DENIAL

Denial is a primitive and very common defense mechanism. To survive an incident that the mind cannot handle, it reacts as if the incident is not happening. Hostages commonly respond by saying or thinking, "This can't be happening to me!" or "This must be a bad dream!" Denial is one stage of coping with an impossible turn of events. These thoughts are actually stress-relieving techniques. Some hostages deny their situation by sleeping.

As time passes, most hostages gradually accept their situation. They find hope in the thought that their fate is not fixed; they begin to view the situation as temporary; and finally, they come to believe they will be rescued soon.

REGRESSION

Regression is the return to a more elementary thought pattern commonly found in children. Like a child, a hostage is in a state of extreme dependence and therefore subject to fright. Unconsciously, the hostage selects a behavior that was successfully used in childhood. The hostage becomes reliant on the hostage-taker, as if the hostage-taker were a parent, providing food, shelter, and protection from the outside world. If this thought pattern is firmly in place, hostages may view authorities as a threat to the "safety" being provided by the hostage-takers.

IDENTIFICATION

Like regression, identifying with the hostage-taker occurs at the unconscious level. The mind seeks to avoid wrath or punishment by mirroring the behaviors and complying with the demands of the hostage-taker.

The Stockholm Syndrome

On August 23, 1973, the quiet, early morning routine of the Credit Bank in Stockholm, Sweden, was destroyed by the sound of submachine gun fire. Four hostages were held for 131 hours: a 25-year old man and three women ranging in age from 21 to 31. They were held by Jan-Erik Olsson, a thief, burglar, and prison escapee. Olsson kept the hostages in an 11-foot by 4-foot crated bank vault, which they came to share with another criminal and former cell mate of Olsson's, Clark Olofsson. Olofsson joined the group after authorities acquiesced to Olsson's demand that his friend be released from prison. Over time, the hostages began to fear the police more than they feared the robbers. In a phone call to Premier Olof Palme, one of the hostages told the premier that the robbers were protecting them from the police. After the hostages were released, they began to question why they didn't hate the robbers, to question why they felt as if Olsson and Olofsson had been the ones to give them their lives back, and to note that they were emotionally indebted to them for this generosity. For weeks after the incident and while under the care of psychiatrists, some of the hostages experienced severely conflicting emotions; they felt fear that Olsson and Olofsson might escape from jail, but they felt no hatred for them. These conflicting psychological emotions resulting from being held hostage has become knows as the Stockholm Syndrome.

Because you are a potential hostage, you must know and understand the Stockholm Syndrome. If taken hostage, you will be able to recognize if it is happening to other hostages, and maybe even if it is happening to you. Observed around the world, the Stockholm Syndrome is an automatic, unconscious emotional response to the trauma of becoming a victim. A positive bond forms, affecting both the hostage and the hostage-taker. The positive emotional bond, which may develop because of the stress of being in a closed room under siege. This bond unites its victims against the outside world. An attitude of "us against them" seems to develop.

The Stockholm Syndrome produces a variety of responses. Minimal responses consist of victims seeing the event through the eyes of their captor or captors. Those deeply influenced respond by recognizing the terrorist for his "gallant act." Responses have also ranged from hostage apathy to actual participation by the hostages in impeding the efforts of rescue forces and negotiation teams. Another response is losing touch with reality and suffering long-term emotional instability.

No one knows how long the syndrome lasts, but the bond seems to be beyond the control of some hostages. They all share common experiences, including positive contact, sympathy for the human qualities of the hostage-takers, and tolerance.

POSITIVE CONTACT

Hostages may develop positive contact with their abductors if they do not have negative experiences (for example, beatings and rapes). Positive contact also develops if there has been a negative experience followed by a positive one. For example, if a hostage is beaten by a "cruel guard" every time he asks for a drink of water, then the cruel guard is replaced by a "kind guard" who gives water freely, the hostage will often establish a positive contact with the latter captor.

HUMAN QUALITIES OF THE HOSTAGE-TAKERS

Hostage-takers may talk about their own mental abuse and physical suffering. They want their hostages to see them as victims of circumstance rather than aggressors. Unfortunately, hostages may sympathize with the hostage-taker and forget that he or she is the one depriving them of their freedom. Once hostages begin to sympathize with the hostage-takers, they may actually support the hostage-takers' cause.

TOLERANCE

Humans have an unconscious limit as to how much we will allow ourselves to be abused or how much we can tolerate. When we are placed in a survival situation, our tolerance for abuse usually increases in order for us to survive.

Coping with Captivity

Coping is a rational mental process used by hostages to deal with and adjust to the problems of a difficult environment. Unlike defense mechanisms, which are mostly unconscious reactions based on personality, coping involves conscious and deliberate thoughts and actions. Coping includes such behaviors as adjusting to living conditions, maintaining dignity and respect, dealing with fear, maintaining mental and physical fitness, and building rapport with captors.

LIVING CONDITIONS

The living conditions hostages are forced to endure vary from incident to incident. Hostages have been held for days in a bus, airliner, or train, where heat or lack of heat and lack of adequate water, food, and toilet facilities were almost unbearable. During the seizure of an office or residence, hostages may be in familiar, comfortable surroundings where they have worked or lived. But kidnap victims are frequently forced to live in makeshift prisons located in attics, basements, or remote hideouts. These prisons may be quite small, and in some cases may prevent the hostage from easily standing or moving around. Sleeping and toilet facilities may be poor, consisting of a cot or mattress and a bucket or tin can for body waste, or a hostage may be forced to soil his living space as well as himself.

The hostage-takers may move you to different holding areas to keep you hidden from authorities. To assist authorities in locating you, you should leave your fingerprints wherever possible in your living area.

DIGNITY AND SELF-RESPECT

Maintaining one's dignity and self-respect can be very difficult, but it is vital to your survival. Your dignity and self-respect may be the keys to retaining your status as a human being in the eyes of the hostage-takers. If you can build empathy while maintaining your dignity, you can potentially lessen the aggression of a captor. Most people cannot inflict pain on another person unless that person becomes dehumanized or turned into a symbol of their hatred.

FEAR

Fear of death is a hostage-taker's most important tool. They use it to control, intimidate, and wear down the hostage and the negotiators. The fear of death is usually greatest during the first few hours of capture. Hostage-takers may induce fear by loading and unloading weapons in the hostage's presence, displaying excesses of temper, resorting to physical abuse, and setting in motion executions that are "mercifully" stopped at the last minute. As this fear subsides, a hostage may begin to hear he "owes" his life to the captors who have "allowed" him to live. Anticipate isolation and terrorist efforts to confuse you. Fear of dying is real, and it can become overwhelming, especially during the early phase of captivity. However, you must try to maintain emotional control in order to stay mentally alert. Fight despair and depression by keeping a positive mental outlook. Remember, although death is a real possibility, most hostages walk away from the ordeal.

PHYSICAL AND MENTAL FITNESS

If abducted, you should develop and maintain a daily physical fitness program. It will help you ward off boredom, and it can reduce stress. Staying physically fit might be the deciding factor if an escape opportunity presents itself and you have to run or walk a considerable distance to reach safety. It may be hard to exercise because of cramped space or physical restraints, but you can run in place or perform isometric exercises. However, you should avoid excessive exercise that could result in injury.

It is important to make some mental link to the outside world. To stimulate your mind, you can read, write, daydream, or use your imagination to build something step-by-step (a house, a car, a piece of furniture). Ask the hostage-takers for reading materials or a radio. If possible, communicate with and try to reassure fellow hostages. If it is your day of worship, mentally walk through the various parts of the worship service. Establish a slow, methodical routine for every task.

Typically, hostage-takers want to keep their hostages alive and well. Eat whatever food is available to maintain your strength. If you need medicine, ask for exactly what you need. If your abductors want you alive, they are not likely to take chances by providing you with the wrong medicine. A side effect of captivity for some hostages is weight loss. Although this may be considerable, it generally does not cause health problems. Hostages may also suffer gastrointestinal upset, including nausea, vomiting, diarrhea, and/or constipation. Although these symptoms can be debilitating, they are usually not life-threatening.

ESTABLISHING RAPPORT

Rapport-building techniques help you make a transition from a faceless symbol who has been dehumanized to one who is human again. However, don't exaggerate your human emotions by begging or crying. An emotional outburst could spread panic and fear among the other hostages and could be viewed as a disgusting display of cowardice by the hostage-takers. You must portray yourself as a person rather than an object by maintaining your dignity, self-respect, and apparent sincerity. You must attempt to establish rapport with your hostage-taker, but you must do so with dignity and self-respect. This rapport may save your life. You should

- Make eye contact with the hostage-takers.
- Greet the hostage-takers and use personal names.
- Smile.
- Talk to the hostage-takers, especially about your family; also, show photos if you have them.
- Determine common interests, e.g., sports or food.
- Listen to the hostage-taker. If he wants to talk about his cause, act interested. You may explain that you might not agree with him but you're interested in his point of view.

- Avoid appearing overly attentive or interested; the hostage-takers may view this as patronizing or insincere.
- Avoid arguing with the hostage-takers. Avoid escalating tensions with words such as "gun," "kill," or "punish" that could cause the hostage-takers to single you out as being argumentative or combative and therefore a threat to the their authority. Bring up neutral topics at critical times to defuse arguments and reduce tensions.
- Avoid emotionally charged topics of religion, economics, and politics.
- Do not refuse favors offered by your captors if doing so will aggravate them or cause further harm to the health and safety of all hostages. However, do not accept favorable treatment at the expense of other hostages. Terrorists commonly employ this controlling tactic to cause division and distrust among the hostage group.

Exploitation of Hostages

Hostages should make reasonable efforts to avoid providing oral or signed confessions, answering questionnaires, making propaganda broadcasts, or conducting news interviews. These actions help terrorist groups further their goals and exploit the media. Interviews broadcast around the world could embarrass the U.S. or host governments. However, if you don't comply with the hostage-takers' requests, you could be tortured or threatened with death. Following are some guidelines:

- You should never mistake pride for inappropriate resistance.
- Keep your temper under control and maintain a polite bearing.
- When being interrogated, take a simple, tenable position and stick with it.
- Give short answers to questions.
- If you are forced to sign or make a statement for the hostage-takers, try to degrade the propaganda, provide minimum information, and avoid making a plea on your behalf.
- Identify your statement as being made in response to the demands of your captors.
- Do not hide your face if the hostage-takers take photographs of the hostages; photos provide authorities with positive identification and information.

Your family also needs to know how to react if you are taken hostage. Typically, terrorists carry radios so they can listen to the news to monitor the world's reaction to the hostage-taking, and so they can receive further instructions from their superiors. Your family should not grant interviews to the media. If confronted by the media for a statement, your family should say that they hope the terrorists will release the hostages and that the ordeal will be over soon.

Releases and Rescue Attempts

Historically, the more time that passes, the better chance a hostage has of being released or rescued. The majority of hostage-taking incidents are resolved by negotiated releases, not rescue attempts. While the passage of time without rescue or release can be depressing, it is actually to your advantage. Time can produce a positive or negative bond between you and your abductors. If the hostage-taker does not abuse you, hours spent together will most likely build rapport, produce positive results, and increase your chances of survival. However, you must also look ahead and plan for your release or rescue. You must remember that if the hostage-takers' demands are not met, they may kill hostages. You must prepare yourself for the potential response from authorities if a hostage is killed. Typically, negotiations cease, and rescue forces move in to rescue hostages.

RELEASES

The moment of imminent release, like the moment of capture, is very dangerous. The hostage-takers, as well as the hostages, are likely to feel threatened and even to panic. The hostage-takers will be extremely nervous during any release phase, especially if negotiations are drawn out. The terrorists will be anxious to evade capture and punishment, and they will fear being double-crossed by the authorities. You need to pay close attention to any instructions the hostage-takers give you when the release takes place. And you must remember not to panic or to run; the hostage-takers may shoot you.

RESCUE ATTEMPTS

During the rescue attempt, both the hostage and the rescue force are in extreme danger. Most hostages who die are killed during rescue attempts. You must be especially alert, cautious, and obedient to instructions if an attempt is imminent or is occurring.

- If possible, position yourself in the safest area you can find, such as under desks, behind chairs, or behind any large object that may provide protection in case of gunfire.
- Avoid being near doors or windows or in open areas.
- If the doors fly open and rescue forces enter, drop to the floor immediately and lie as flat as possible. Do not move, do not say anything, and do not attempt to pick up a weapon or help the rescuers.

Rescue forces have no idea whether you are friend or foe. Any movement you make could result in injury or death to you or your fellow hostages. It could also distract members of the rescue force, which, in turn, could lead to injuries or deaths among the rescuers. During a rescue operation at Entebbe, Uganda, a female hostage threw her hands up in a natural gesture of joy as the rescue forces came bursting in. Unfortunately, the rescue forces shot her. Once the rescue forces are in control, you might be handled roughly and ordered up against the wall. You will probably be handcuffed, searched, and possibly gagged and/or blindfolded until everyone is positively identified.

AFTER THE RELEASE

Once you are safely in the hands of the authorities, remember to cooperate fully with them, especially if others are still being held. As soon as you can, write down everything you can remember: guard location, weapons and explosives description and placement, and any other information that might help rescue forces.

After your release, you must prepare yourself for the aftermath. The news media will want an interview immediately, and you will be in no condition to provide intelligent, accurate responses. Do not make comments to the news media until you have been debriefed by proper U.S. authorities and have been cleared to talk to reporters. You should say only that you are grateful to be alive and thankful for being released. You should not say anything that could harm fellow hostages who may still be in captivity. You must not say anything that is sympathetic to the terrorist cause or that might result in increased support for them.

Upon release, many hostages feel guilty for not having conducted themselves in a heroic manner. Emotional turmoil is common. Some may feel angry because they feel that their government did not do enough to protect them.

Remember that a government's unwillingness to make concessions to terrorists discourages future acts of terrorism and sends a message to all terrorists worldwide. When ransoms for captives of terrorists have been paid by governments, these payments have usually been used by terrorists to increase their status and capability to continue terrorist acts. A government's refusal to give in to terrorists does not mean that your life had no value. It is the policy of the United States that when Americans are abducted overseas, the United States will continue to cultivate international cooperation to combat terrorism and to secure the safe release of the hostages.

CONCLUSION

CALM PREVAILS

Today, terrorists have reached new levels of organization, sophistication, and violence. Most Americans first began to realize the danger when we learned of the horrendous attacks of 9/11; from then on, the words "September 11," for most of us, conjured images of burning towers of steel and glass, coupled with feelings of fear and helplessness. Since then, bombings in Bali and elsewhere, regular news warnings of new plots, and a continuous state of world upheaval have combined to leave many people feeling insecure and unsafe.

The tactics and techniques of terrorists are always changing and will continue to present challenges to safety the world over. American citizens, along with our law enforcement agencies and government organizations—in particular, the newly formed Department of Homeland Security—must remain diligent in applying the proper protective measures. Our goal is to stop terrorist attacks before they happen. All Americans should begin a process of learning about potential threats so we are better prepared to react during an attack.

But we do not have to be paralyzed by fear. While there is no way to predict what will happen, or what your personal circumstances will be if and when something does happen, this book, with its many suggestions on how to prepare for almost any eventuality, can help. Of course, this guide will not ensure immunity from terrorism, but by practicing these techniques and proven security habits, the possibility of becoming a target will be reduced. Defensive awareness and personal security regarding terrorism are everyone's responsibility. Constant awareness can help protect all citizens from acts of terrorism.

It is our hope that after reading this guide, you are less anxious about the threat of terrorism on U.S. soil. We believe that the key to safety is awareness: the more you know, the less you will fear; the better prepared you can be, the less likely you are to be bogged down a sense of hopelessness. Remember, the government is here to help; local, regional, and federal law enforcement is your ally in the war on terror.

As our national leaders continually remind us, our best course is to persevere in our way of life. We must not let our enemies terrorize us. We must be alert and we must be prepared, but that should not stop us from going about our daily lives. If we live in fear, then the terrorists have already won. We can beat them by living our lives to the fullest while taking appropriate precautions. *Be prepared.*

APPENDICES

HELPFUL ORGANIZATIONS

U.S. Department of Homeland Security

The vanguard in the War on Terror

http://www.dhs.gov

http://www.whitehouse.gov/homeland

Contact information in your state

http://www.whitehouse.gov/homeland/contactmap.html

http://www.ready.gov/useful_state.html

Department of State

Travel warnings, crisis awareness and preparedness, emergencies abroad, passports

http://www.state.gov

Detailed information on U.S. embassies and consulates abroad, by continent

http://usembassy.state.gov/

U.S. Department of State
2201 C Street, NW
Washington, DC 20520
(202) 647-4000

Federal Bureau of Investigation

http://www.fbi.gov

FBI's counterterrorism site

http://www.fbi.gov/terrorinfo/counterrorism/waronterrorhome.htm

Field offices by state

http://www.fbi.gov/contact/fo/territory.htm

Federal Bureau of Investigation
J. Edgar Hoover Building
935 Pennsylvania Avenue, NW
Washington, D.C. 20535-0001

Centers for Disease Control and Prevention

Terrorism and public health

http://www.bt.cdc.gov
(800) 311-3435

Travelers' health

http://www.cdc.gov/travel/
(877) FYI-TRIP

HELPFUL ORGANIZATIONS *cont'd*

U.S. Department of Health and Human Services
http://www.hhs.gov

Information on bioterrorism and homeland security
http://www.hhs.gov/disasters/index.shtml

The U.S. Department of Health and Human Services
200 Independence Avenue, SW
Washington, D.C. 20201
(202) 619-0257 or (877) 696-6775

Poison Control Center
http://www.aapcc.org/findyour.htm
(800) 222-1222

American Red Cross
http://www.redcross.org/

For the chapter nearest you
http://www.redcross.org/where/where.html

American Red Cross National Headquarters
431 18th Street, NW
Washington, DC 20006
(202) 303-4498

The Humane Society of the United States
Information on animal care and safety
2100 L Street, NW
Washington, D.C. 20037
Attn: Disaster Services Program
(202) 452-1100

EMERGENCY SURVIVAL KIT CHECKLIST

Chapter Three explores the reasons for putting together an emergency survival kit and lists the items you will need to include. A good way to make sure you have everything you need is to photocopy this handy checklist and mark off each item as you complete your kit(s).

Water

- [ ] One gallon/person/day (minimum)

Food

At least a three-day supply for each person:

- [ ] Ready-to-eat canned meats, fruits, and vegetables
- [ ] Protein or fruit bars
- [ ] Dry cereal or granola
- [ ] Peanut butter
- [ ] Dried fruit
- [ ] Nuts
- [ ] Crackers
- [ ] Canned juices
- [ ] Non-perishable pasteurized milk
- [ ] High-energy foods
- [ ] Vitamins
- [ ] Food for infants
- [ ] Baby formula
- [ ] Comfort and stress foods

Clean Air

- [ ] Breathing masks for each person, or layers of cloth that can serve as masks
- [ ] Heavyweight plastic garbage bags or plastic sheeting, pre-cut to seal off your "safe room"

- [ ] Duct tape
- [ ] Scissors
- [ ] Portable air purifier

First Aid Kit

- [ ] Two pairs of sterile gloves
- [ ] Sterile dressings
- [ ] Adhesive bandages
- [ ] Cleansing agent/soap
- [ ] Antibiotic towelettes
- [ ] Antibiotic ointment
- [ ] Burn ointment
- [ ] Thermometer
- [ ] Medicine dropper
- [ ] Eye wash solution
- [ ] Your daily prescription medications
- [ ] Prescribed medical supplies
- [ ] Scissors
- [ ] Tweezers
- [ ] Tube of petroleum jelly or other lubricant
- [ ] Potassium iodide
- [ ] Aspirin or non-aspirin pain reliever
- [ ] Anti-diarrhea medication
- [ ] Antacid
- [ ] Syrup of Ipecac
- [ ] Laxative
- [ ] Activated charcoal

Special Needs Items

- [ ] Diapers
- [ ] Baby bottles
- [ ] Powdered milk
- [ ] Medications
- [ ] Moist towelettes
- [ ] Diaper rash ointment

- [ ] Contact lenses and supplies
- [ ] Extra eyeglasses
- [ ] List of doctors and emergency contacts
- [ ] List of prescription medications
- [ ] List of allergies
- [ ] Denture needs
- [ ] Hearing-aid batteries
- [ ] Extra wheelchair batteries or other special equipment
- [ ] A list of the style and serial numbers of medical devices you use
- [ ] Copies of medical insurance and Medicare cards
- [ ] Extra oxygen

Basic Supplies

- [ ] Cash or traveler's checks, change
- [ ] Flashlight and extra batteries
- [ ] Battery-powered radio and extra batteries
- [ ] Map of the area
- [ ] Whistle
- [ ] Paper towels
- [ ] Moist towelettes

Food-Related Needs

- [ ] Manual can opener
- [ ] Mess kits, or paper cups, paper plates, and plastic utensils
- [ ] Aluminum foil
- [ ] Plastic storage containers

Clothing

At least one complete change of warm clothing and shoes per person:

- [ ] Jacket or coat
- [ ] Long pants
- [ ] Long-sleeved shirt
- [ ] Sturdy shoes

- [ ] Hat
- [ ] Gloves

Bedding Needs

- [ ] Sleeping bag or warm blanket for each person
- [ ] Tube tent for every two people

Tools

- [ ] Non-electric can opener
- [ ] Utility knife
- [ ] Fire extinguisher
- [ ] Pliers
- [ ] Compass
- [ ] Matches in a waterproof container
- [ ] Signal flare
- [ ] Paper
- [ ] Pencil
- [ ] Shut-off wrench

Sanitation

- [ ] Toilet paper
- [ ] Moist towelettes
- [ ] Feminine supplies
- [ ] Personal hygiene items
- [ ] Plastic garbage bags and ties
- [ ] Plastic bucket with tight lid
- [ ] Disinfectant
- [ ] Household chlorine bleach

Documents

- [ ] Copies of family records such as identification, bank account records, insurance policies, property documents in a portable waterproof container
- [ ] Emergency reference material such as a first aid book or a printout of this information

IMPORTANT DOCUMENTS CHECKLIST

It is sensible to have all your important family documents organized during the best of times; in uncertain times, you'll want to make it a priority. Use this checklist to assemble your documents and to make sure that all of them are up to date. You may want to keep some original documents in a safety deposit box, fireproof safe, or another secure location; if so, keep copies handy so you can access them easily and take them with you, if necessary.

Medical

- ☐ Health records for each family member, including one page for each person with a brief history of any major medical conditions or episodes, vaccination records, and doctors' contact information
- ☐ List of special needs for any family member (e.g., disability, pregnancy, allergy, etc.)
- ☐ List of medications needed by family members
- ☐ Health insurance information
- ☐ Name and address of family dentist

Financial

- ☐ Bank name, address, and phone number

  Checking Account ______________________________

  Savings Account ______________________________

  Other Accounts ______________________________
- ☐ Retirement accounts name, address, phone numbers

- [ ] Credit card account numbers and expiration dates

    Account ______________________________

    Account ______________________________

    Account ______________________________

Family

- [ ] Birth certificates
- [ ] Marriage certificate
- [ ] Divorce decree
- [ ] Passport
- [ ] Citizenship papers
- [ ] Adoption papers
- [ ] Social Security cards
- [ ] Driver's licenses

General Household

- [ ] State and federal tax records
- [ ] Fire/homeowner's/renter's insurance
- [ ] Life insurance
- [ ] U.S. Savings Bonds, stocks, securities deeds or mortgages
- [ ] Car title and registration
- [ ] Automobile insurance
- [ ] Will
- [ ] Location of extra set of house keys and car keys
- [ ] Names and descriptions of any pets
- [ ] Veterinarian's name, address, and phone number

VEHICLE EMERGENCY SUPPLIES

In general, you should keep your car fully equipped with supplies that could be useful in an emergency.

- Blanket
- Booster cables
- Extra clothing and footwear
- Fire extinguisher
- First aid kit with first aid manual
- Flashlight and batteries
- Maps
- Matches and a "survival" candle in a tin can (to warm hands, heat a drink, or use as an emergency light)
- Non-perishable high-energy foods (raisins, granola bars, etc).
- Sand
- Shovel
- Solar, wind-up, or battery-powered radio
- Tool kit
- Bottled water
- Warning light or reflectors; flares

IMPORTANT PHONE NUMBERS

You should keep these numbers handy; post them by the phone, and keep a separate copy in your wallet. Copy them for each member of the family.

- Police
- Fire
- Ambulance
- Poison information
- Out-of-town contact person
- Doctor
- Cell phone number of each family member
- Workplace of each family member
- School of each family member

Note: Keep e-mail addresses for each family member handy, too.

FAMILY EMERGENCY WALLET CARD

These emergency card templates are useful for each family member to carry in a wallet, handbag, or knapsack. Make a copy for each family member then take them to a local copy shop to be laminated.

Family Emergency Card

Name ______________________________

Address ______________________________

Phones (**H**) ______________ (**W**) ______________

(**C**) ______________________________

Emergency contact person ______________________________

Phones (**H**) ______________ (**W**) ______________

(**C**) ______________________________

E-mail ______________________________

Emergency meeting plan A

Where ______________________________

When ______________________________

Contact numbers ______________________________

Emergency meeting plan B

Where ______________________________

When ______________________________

Contact numbers ______________________________

MEDICAL INFORMATION WALLET CARD

Although your family records contain complete medical histories for each family member, these cards, with basic information, will be useful in an emergency.

Medical Information Card

Name ______________________________

Address ______________________________

Phones (**H**) ______________ (**W**) ______________

Physician's name ______________________________

Phone ______________________________

Emergency contact ______________________________

Phone ______________________________

Patient Information

Date of Birth ___________ Blood type ___________

Allergies ______________________________

Conditions ______________________________

Medications ______________________________

Special needs ______________________________

Health insurance ______________________________

INDEX

Page numbers in italics refer to illustrations.

INDEX

INDEX

INDEX

NOTES

These pages are provided to give you a place to begin creating your family survival plan. Some ideas for how to use them:

- Outline your unique family "threat profile" by examining the details of where you live, work, and travel; use it to identify the particular threats you need to prepare for
- Assemble necessary information on each family member (including those who may live apart from you, such as grown children or elderly parents or relatives)
- Map out household exits and/or safe rooms
- Map your neighborhood and identify potential family meeting places
- Note your pet safety plans
- List potential local and out-of-town contact people
- Note any questions you may wish to ask of local authorities, family physicians, or other sources of information

NOTES

NOTES

NOTES

NOTES

NOTES